# WOMEN of the FRONTIER ARMY

## True Tales of the Old West

by

### Charles L. Convis

**Watercolor Cover by Mary Anne Convis**

**PIONEER PRESS INC., CARSON CITY, NEVADA**

Library of Congress Catalog Card Number: 96-68502

ISBN 1-892156-15-6

# CONTENTS

## ILLUSTRATIONS

# ARMY WIFE, INTERPRETER, INTREPID SCOUT

A Paiute girl, born sometime in 1844, was named Thocmetony (Shell Flower). Her father, Winnemucca, was a headman in the tribe, and whites called the girl Sarah Winnemucca. Most of Sarah's adult life involved the army. She married a lieutenant but soon left him. Nine years later she married a recently-discharged soldier. There may have been other army husbands, but it was a time when laws prohibited interracial marriages, and records are hard to find.

But Sarah's most important involvement with the army was her service as a scout in the Bannock War of 1878. Just one year had passed since the Nez Perce had thrilled the nation with their fight for freedom, and the Bannocks of present Idaho, fed up with disgraceful treatment by thieving Indian agents, decided they'd go on the attack.

Sarah had been employed as an interpreter at Fort McDermit in Nevada since 1869. Besides translating words between the army and the Paiutes, she tried to describe each side's cultural attitudes and social expectations. Only in this way, she thought, could her people and the whites learn to live peacefully with each other. She knew from her contact with army officers that most of them sympathized with the Indians and thought their complaints justified.

Sarah was sometimes a gambler, a carouser, a drinker, and even a fist fighter. In June, 1878, she rode through some of the roughest country in the West to reach her father and his small band of about seventy-five, whom the Bannocks had taken prisoner after confiscating their guns and horses. Then Sarah engineered a thrilling nighttime escape, rescuing her father's band from a Bannock village of four hundred, fifty warriors. She persuaded the Paiutes that the army would protect them and provide rations.

General Oliver O. Howard and his officers could hardly believe what Sarah had done. Her two hundred, twenty-three mile ride from ten A. M. on June 13 to 5:30 P. M. on June 15 matched in danger, difficulty, and determination earlier legendary rides by John C. Fremont, Marcus Whitman, and Portugee Phillips. Howard hired her on the spot as his scout. He also hired her sister-in-law, Mattie, to help interpret.

And what a pair Sarah and the general made! Howard lost an arm and gained a Medal of Honor in the Civil War. President Johnson put this devoutly religious officer at the head of the Freedmen's Bureau, where he made sure that the blessings of emancipation were not lost to former slaves. President Grant sent him to the Southwest where he successfully ended the long, bitter dispute between settlers and Geronimo's Apaches. The field leader during most of the Nez Perce War, Howard now had another war on his hands.

In referring to her daring rescue ride, Sarah said, "I went for the government when the officers could not get, for love or money, an Indian or a white man to go."

Howard characterized her statement as rather boastful, but "nevertheless, perfectly true."

Sarah's report of what she had seen in the Bannock camp led Howard to change his whole plan of defense, a change that he said proved to be for the best. First he sent Sarah and her sister, with an escort of officers, to his headquarters. Sarah was furious; she wanted to ride at once to the attack!

Howard did not want to kill Indians. His goal was to bring them back to their reservations and allay the fears of white settlers, often prone to act hastily out of fear and revenge.

With the continuous assistance of Sarah, he was able to end the war with very few fatalities. Unfortunately, one of those was Sarah's sister-in-law, who was thrown from her horse while the two women were riding at break neck speed through rough country

The close association between Sarah Winnemucca and General Howard was similar to the one between Sacajawea and Captains Meriwether Lewis and William Clark of seventy-five years before. Howard, in describing Sarah's assistance, said, "She did our government great service, and if I could tell you a tenth part of all she willingly did to help the white settlers and her own people to live peacefully together I am sure you would think, as I do, that the name of Thocmetony should have a place beside the name of Pocahontas in the history of our country."

Sarah's autobiography, *Life Among the Paiutes,* was the first book written in English by a Native American. Sacajawea has more monuments and memorials than any other woman of America. But both are buried in unmarked graves.

Within a year or two, each woman will be honored in a very visible place in Washington, D. C. Nevada will unveil a statue of Sarah Winnemucca and North Dakota one of Sacajawea in our nation's Statuary Hall. This writer's wife—this book's cover artist—is co-chair of the Nevada Sarah Winnemucca Statue Project.

Suggested reading: Oliver O. Howard, *My Life and Experiences among our Hostile Indians* (Hartford: A. D. Worthington Co., 1907).

4

# HEROINE OF FORT BROWN

When the 7<sup>TH</sup> U. S. Infantry was stopped by Mexican guerillas at the Arroyo Colorado, about thirty-five miles north of the Rio Grande in early 1846, Sarah marched to the front and announced: "General, lend me a pair of pants and I'll wade the river and whip every Mexican scoundrel that dares show his face."

The general was "Old Rough and Ready" Zachary Taylor, hero of the Seminole War in Florida. Commanding over half the troops in the United States Army, he was marching south to teach the Mexicans a lesson. Sarah, now the cook for the regimental officers' mess, had been a camp follower in Florida and had followed Taylor to Texas. Rumored to be in love with him, she was half the age of the general, who had been married for thirty-six years.

Sarah, of course, had to have a husband in the 7<sup>th</sup> in order to travel with it. We don't know his name, but he was traveling down the coast in a boat while Sarah marched with her troops.

Sarah was six feet, two inches tall with flaming red hair and bright blue eyes. She drove the donkey pulling her cart of equipment and supplies like the loudest teamster, and she filled out her dress like the voluptuous women of the New Orleans waterfront.

She was born Sarah Bourgette in Tennessee, but from the time she appeared in southwestern history until her death twenty years later, she was always called the Great Western, after a steamship of that name, famous for its size. The well built Amazon also had a heart filled with courage and a soul filled with sympathy. Soldiers, frontiersmen, and miners spoke of her in their bivouacs, cabins, and camps with affection and awe.

The guerillas scattered, and the 7<sup>th</sup> reached the Rio Grande to start building a fort. The Mexicans watched and waited. They thought the Americans had been invading their homeland ever since crossing the Nueces. Texas, recently annexed to the United States, had never claimed land south of Corpus Christi. General Francisco Mejia, commander at Matamoros, said America's "perfidy would forever stain the character for virtue falsely attributed to its people." The deep waters of the Rio Grande would be the sepulchre of any foe who tried to cross.

The Mexicans started shelling the fort on May 3. The dozen or so women with the regiment were ordered to safety in an underground magazine. The Great Western refused to go. She had started breakfast over an open fire, and she finished it. Then she served the artillerymen who could not leave their guns. She kept this up, three meals a day, for a week. Once, when the cause looked hopeless, she asked for a musket and ammunition, saying she would fight with her soldiers to the end. Her "husband" was still at the supply depot on the coast; he never joined his regiment in the field.

All told, the Mexicans fired 2700 rounds into the fort, almost sixty for each defender. When she was not cooking, the Great Western served as a nurse. One soldier said, "She exhibited great courage, and the most cool, daring intrepidity. The cannon balls, bullets, and shot, those sure messengers of death, were falling thick and fast around her. She continued to administer to the wants of the wounded and dying; at last the siege became so hot that a bullet passed through her bonnet and another through her bread tray while she was preparing some refreshments for the men."

A few days after the battle, at a dinner party in Matamoros, Braxton Bragg, a lieutenant who would later be a Confederate general in the Civil War, led a toast to the heroine of Fort Brown. "The men leaped up, drank the toast with thunderous cheers and teary eyes, and hurled their glasses at the walls."

A veteran of the siege referred to her "courageous spirit which bore her through all the trials of this bombardment, but whose masculine hardihood was softened by the gentleness of a female heart."

Congress declared war and asked for 50,000 volunteers. Men from all over the young nation streamed south to be part of its first experience in a foreign war. Strangers to the tropical climate and not trained in field sanitation, many soldiers fell to yellow fever, small pox, dysentery, and cholera. The Great Western was busy.

In February, 1847, the Americans fought at Buena Vista, southwest of Monterrey. Outnumbered but not outgeneraled—Zachary Taylor against Santa Anna—they won the bloodiest battle to be fought by the United States Army before the Civil War. It was the last battle for Taylor and the Great Western. The 7th Infantry had been moved to another part of Mexico, but the Great Western, wanting to stay with her general, had taken another husband in the 2d Dragoons. She cooked, made cartridges, and nursed the wounded, carrying some of them from the battlefield during the hottest part of the fight. Once, a volunteer soldier was being chased by two Mexicans. As he ran through the Great Western's kitchen, he shouted that the army was being cut to pieces. She hit him between the eyes and knocked him down. "You damned son of a bitch," she said, "there ain't Mexicans enough in Mexico to whip old Taylor. You just spread that report and I'll beat you to death!"

Late in 1847, the Great Western was operating the American House in Monterrey. Popular with American troops, it was a combination saloon and restaurant. Her saloons and hotels were as well known in the army as her battlefield exploits. Her usual charges were six dollars a week board and room, five dollars to board a horse.

The war ended in February, 1848, and the Great Western said goodbye to Old Rough and Ready. He returned to the United States to be elected president. She joined a battalion of dragoons marching across Mexico to California. A discharged private, hired as a wagon master, said she rode up with her three servants at the head of a three-wagon train and asked for permission to join. Told that she would have to marry a dragoon to be mustered in as a laundress, she said, "I'll marry the whole squadron." Then she rode back and forth in front of the troops, saying, "Who wants a wife with fifteen thousand dollars and the biggest leg in Mexico! Come on, my beauties, don't all speak at once—who is the lucky man?"

She married a man named Davis in E Company and joined the expedition. When Davis said he wanted a clergyman to tie the knot, she laughed and said, "Bring your blanket to my tent tonight and I will learn you to tie a knot that will satisfy you, I reckon."

A few days after they left Chihuahua, they met a trading party from Santa Fe. It included a man of "remarkable size and strength." When the Great Western saw him taking a bath, she "conceived a violent passion for his gigantic proportions." Sampson became the willing captive of Delilah, who "kicked Davis out of her affections and tent and established her elephantine lover in full possession without further ceremony."

Early in 1849 the Great Western was operating a saloon across the river from El Paso del Norte. She was always glad to see army officers who stopped in. One wrote, "Never was anyone more delighted at the sight of American officers. Her masculine arms lifted us one after the other off our feet."

John "Rip" Ford, famous Texas ranger and Indian fighter, said, "She could whip any man, fair fight or foul, could shoot a pistol better than anyone in the region, and at blackjack could out play (or out cheat) the slickest professional gambler."

The Great Western's final husband was Albert J. Bowman, whom she married at Fort Yuma sometime before 1860. She died on December 22, 1866, was given a military funeral, and was buried in the Fort Yuma post cemetery. When Fort Yuma was closed in 1890, her remains, along with those of 158 soldiers, were re-buried at the Presidio in San Francisco. The soldiers were buried in a mass grave; she got her own private plot. Her general, from whom she never ventured far while attached to the army, rests near Louisville, Kentucky, almost a continent away.

Suggested reading: Charles L. Convis, "The Great Western" in *True West* (September, 1989).

# EARLY ARMY LIFE IN TEXAS

Teresa Vielé was the first woman to publish an account of army life in the West, and one of the few to write about army life in Texas. Born Teresa Griffon in New York in 1831, her father was a lawyer and her mother a writer. In 1850 the nineteen-year-old girl married Lieutenant Egbert Vielé of the army. After recruiting duty in Burlington, Vermont, he was assigned in 1852 to the 1st Infantry stationed at Ringgold Barracks on the lower Rio Grande.

They traveled by steamer with stops at Havana, New Orleans, Galveston and Indianola before reaching Fort Brown, the center of action at the beginning of the recent war against Mexico. Their carriage passed the scenes of the Battles of Palo Alto and Reseca de la Palma on their way from the steamer landing to the fort.

Teresa noted the primitive life of the Mexicans. In one thatched straw hut built on four poles she saw an old crone picking vermin out of the hair of a young girl, while another girl was doing the same to the old woman's hair. Teresa commented that the performance displayed more vitality than one usually sees among Mexicans.

Brownsville, adjacent to the fort, had no church; only one wandering Presbyterian preacher. Teresa obviously didn't consider Catholics in her biased survey. She expressed respect for the original priests who had brought religion and civilization to the country, but she said it would be hard to find a "more dissolute, carnal, gambling, jolly set of wine-bibbers" than the Mexican priests of that day. Although the priests were well educated and agreeable, she thought they ruled the ignorant peasantry with a strong mixture of superstition and dread.

The soldiers waited several weeks in Brownsville for their supplies to come on another steamer. While they waited, Teresa saw an enlisted man drummed out of the army for theft. His head was shaved and all his military clothes and identification taken from him except his pantaloons, bearing the red stripe for artillery. At evening parade he was called before the ranks and dismissed from the service, the officer of the day reading the crime and the penalty in full. Then, while the band played *Poor Old Soldier,* he walked three times around the parade ground. The corporal and the sergeant of the guard followed closely, prodding him along with bayonets.

When the miscreant passed the officer's quarters he shouted impertinently that they should take up a subscription and buy him a wig. Two bayonet thrusts promptly reminded him to show more respect. Then he was ejected from the fort's gate, probably, thought Teresa, to go off and buy himself a wig.

Halfway up the Rio Grande to Ringgold Barracks Teresa's party passed Edinburgh, Texas. Teresa, with her quick judgments, thought it had been settled by a thieving Scotsman who named it for his home. Not far upstream the boat came under fire from what the passengers thought were Comanches. No one was hurt on the boat. They returned fire and the attack stopped.

Teresa thought that Comanches would never be civilized, their principal food was raw meat, and "actual extermination" was the only remedy for their scourge. In passing a Mexican village, Teresa described the women as "rather slovenly, and consequently far from attractive, although at a little distance they look well." She thought Saturday night baths were unheard of among the babies.

Ringgold Barracks, four days upriver from Brownsville, was located on a high bluff. Its low, whitewashed, modern buildings surrounded a level drill ground. The officers had intelligence and polish that would have been appreciated in the world's most elegant salons. The only women she saw were Mexicans and camp followers.

Teresa lost her middle-aged maid to the marriage proposal of a blacksmith in Brownsville. The maid was replaced by a black man. With a soldier delegated to cook and a drummer boy to wash dishes, Teresa was freed of most household responsibilities.

Rio Grande City, a village of a thousand, was located a mile from the post. It had been settled four years before by Henry Clay Davis, who ran away from his Kentucky home at fifteen. After killing a man on a Mississippi River steamboat, he fled to Arkansas and made his way to Texas to serve in its revolution from Mexico. After Texas joined the United States, Davis again began wandering, settling on the lower Rio Grande.

Teresa described Davis as a true specimen of the Texan, "tall and athletic, yet his delicately cut features, carefully trimmed mustache, and *air distingué,* bespoke rather the modern carpet knight than the hero and pioneer of the wilderness." Association with Mexicans had given Texans "a peculiar style of manner, a mixture of western frankness and the stateliness of the Spaniard — a low-toned voice, and a deference mixed with assurance."

In the Texan, Teresa thought, "are combined the raciness of the Kentuckian, the Creole impetuosity of Louisiana, with the reckless heart-in-hand spirit of the Southwest. They follow different callings, from the scout to the office holder under the government, but there exist no false distinctions among them. A man stands simply on his own merits. The word blasé or the idea conveyed by it is unknown. Fresh as nature around them, their hearts beat true to the call of friendship, and respect for women seems an innate principle, while daring and bravery are no second nature, but nature itself."

The summer months passed quickly. The heat would have been too much except for the delightfully cool nights. Teresa amused herself by collecting wild animals. By September she had a small zoo enclosed in a high fence of interlaced brush behind her house. It included a fawn, two goats, a flock of doves, a brood of chickens, a parrot, four dogs of different breeds, mocking birds, orioles, and a tiger cub, of which she was mortally afraid. She always kept the animal chained, and her black servant fed it raw meat.

After about a year in Texas, Teresa and her husband returned to New York on a leave of absence. Again, it was a water journey, but by a different route. Going down river to Brownsville, they took a steamer to New Orleans. Then they took river boats up the Mississippi and Ohio Rivers to Cincinnati. From there they traveled to Lake Erie and across it to Buffalo, then through Albany to New York City.

Ringgold Barracks soon became a prominent army post in Texas. Both Robert E. Lee and Ulysses S. Grant, at one time opposing each other in the Civil War, served there before the war.

Twenty years after returning to New York, the Vielés divorced. Teresa and their eight-year-old son Egbert moved to Paris, France. Later, Teresa returned to the United States and kidnapped their youngest daughter Emily from her ex-husband. They returned to Paris, where Teresa lived the rest of her life. She is buried there. Her son became a leading author and poet in France.

This intelligent but very opinionated woman left us a charming description of army life in early Texas.

Suggested reading: Teresa Griffin Vielé, *Following the Drum* (Lincoln: University of Nebraska Press, 1984).

# LONG WEDDING TRIP

**M**elissa Burton Coray's wedding trip was two thousand miles long and lasted six months. The eighteen-year-old girl had been married just four days when her husband joined Company B of a battalion of Mormon volunteers that President Polk wanted for the protection of southern California during the War against Mexico.

Eight years before, Melissa's family had fled Canada for Ohio to escape religious persecution. But the United States was no better, and now they had moved on to Iowa, still looking for a place to worship peacefully. Twenty-three-year-old Will Coray had been courting Melissa for three years, and she was so proud that he was recruited as a sergeant, and she had been accepted as one of the company's four laundresses. Now they could march into the future together! And showing their loyalty to the United States might stop the persecution they had all suffered. Melissa and Will sure hoped so; they wanted their children to have religious freedom.

Melissa and Will signed up at Mt. Pisgah, Iowa, and then traveled one hundred thirty miles west to Council Bluffs, where the battalion started its march on July 20, 1846. Anguished cries of wives, mothers, and children followed the men as they marched away, but Melissa and Will were thankful to be together.

Three days later the 500-man battalion had its first death when Sam Boley of Company B died during the night at their camp in northwest Missouri. The marchers had taken only a little flour and parched corn with them, not wanting to deprive their families of any more food, and most were hungry. At this time, nine-year-old Charles Colton walked in to camp. He had run away from home to be with his father. They let him stay.

One of the few references to Melissa's duties as a laundress came before they reached Fort Leavenworth. She earned eighteen and a half cents doing laundry for Samuel Rogers.

The men were issued tents and rifles at Leavenworth. They also received their uniform allowances in advance, forty-two dollars each. Most sent the money back to their families rather than spend it on uniforms. Apostle Parley Pratt led a small party that returned to Council Bluffs with the money. The only thing uniform about the soldiers' clothing was a white belt.

Each company was allowed to buy a baggage wagon and a four-mule team, and each mess was issued a kettle, frying pan, coffee pot, and five days' rations. Will also bought a two-horse carriage. He and another man had bought two horses from a settler a few days before.

After two weeks of training, Company B and two other companies left the fort for the seven hundred-mile march to Santa Fe. They followed the

Santa Fe Trail, taking the Cimarron cutoff. The remaining companies of the battalion would follow when ready.

Four days later a hurricane hit. The Coray carriage was blown into a gully. Just before it crashed, Will grabbed Melissa and got her out.

Ten days out of Leavenworth, about eighty men were sick and convalescing. They learned that their commanding officer, sick and left behind at the fort, had died. The men wanted Jefferson Hunt, a Mormon, to take command, but regular army Lieutenant Andrew Smith came out from Leavenworth and took over.

The first woman—a teamster's wife—died on August 27, and her husband died three days later.

On September 15 they turned into the Cimarron Cutoff, and a guard of ten men took all the sick men, women, and children straight ahead to Pueblo. This included ten of the original thirty-six women.

Sterling Price, commanding a regiment of Volunteer Missouri Cavalry, was traveling on ahead. Taking the Cimarron Cutoff meant that supplies could not be replenished at Bent's Fort, so Lieutenant Smith sent a message ahead for Price to send back provisions. Price said he wasn't hauling supplies for Mormons. Smith replied that he'd turn the Mormons loose on the Missourians and support them with artillery. Price sent the supplies.

The next day another man died.

The cutoff was very dry. On September 18 they had to drive buffalo out of a stagnant pond to get drinking water. "The water was like a thick gruel of buffalo urine, bugs, and rainwater. The men rushed to it, lay down, and sucked and strained the water through their teeth to keep from swallowing bugs." Then they filled their canteens. Several were soon sick.

Lieutenant Smith tried to train his men, but it was impossible without proper shoes, food, and water.

The battalion reached Santa Fe on October 12, where Colonel Philip St. George Cooke of the army's dragoons took command. Besides getting the men to California, he wanted to locate a wagon road from the Rio Grande to San Diego.

Colonel Cooke wanted to send all the women and children back to Pueblo. After discussions with General Doniphan, commanding in New Mexico, five, including Melissa, were allowed to continue with the battalion.

South of Albuquerque, a new guide joined them. He was Jean Baptiste Charbonneau, a skilled mountain man who as a baby had journeyed to the Pacific Ocean with his mother, Sacajawea. From Elephant Butte on —seven hundred miles—the wagons were the first to travel the route. At that point a third detachment of sick, including one woman, were returned to Pueblo.

Encountering wolves, bears, wild bulls that charged the soldiers,

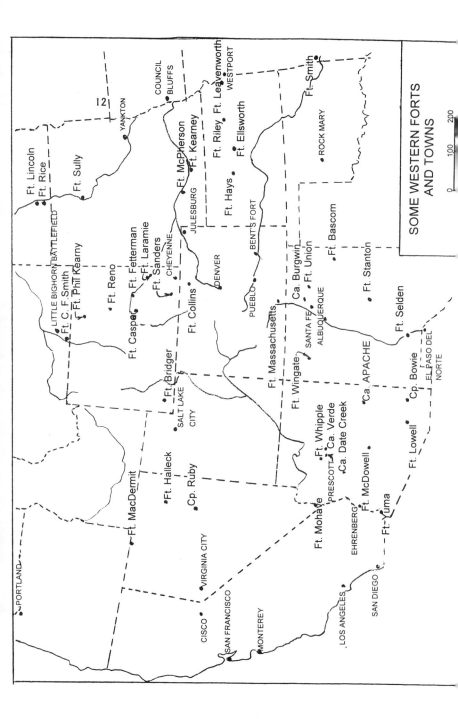

SOME WESTERN FORTS
AND TOWNS

0    100    200

traveling once for forty miles without water and through snowstorms, and burying five more men, they reached California to learn that the war there was over. They reached San Diego on January 29, 1847.

The battalion was ordered to Mission San Luis Rey in case hostilities were resumed. On March 15, B company was ordered back to San Diego and the other four companies to Los Angeles.

Lydia Hunter, wife of B Company's captain and a laundress in his company, bore a son on April 20 and died six days later. Melissa was now the only women left in the company. She was pregnant, giving her additional worries of her own.

The company was ordered to Los Angeles in July, where, on the 16th, with their year of service completed the battalion was discharged. Each man kept his rifle and twenty-one rounds of ammunition. No one got an allowance for travel back to Council Bluffs. Eighty-one men volunteered to serve another six months.

The discharged soldiers wanted to get back to their people, who were moving west toward the Valley of the Great Salt Lake when the soldiers marched away back in July. Some traveled north up the Central Valley. Others, including Melissa and Will, followed the Mission Trail northwest along the coast. When they reached Monterey, Melissa and Will stayed until their son was born on October 2.

Will expressed his joy nine days later in a letter to a comrade in San Francisco: "I am the biggest man in all Israel. I have the greatest boy you ever want anywhere, and I am coming up to show him just as soon as the woman gets well enough."

Melissa recovered, but the baby died. They moved on to San Francisco where Will found employment as a freighter. Melissa took long walks along the beach, usually bringing back sticks for their fire, a habit she had learned on their long march.

The Bay Area Mormons organized a branch of their church in December.

News of the January, 1848, gold discovery had just reached San Francisco when the discharged soldiers began their return journey. They saw people washing out gold but did not stop long as they were anxious to reach Salt Lake.

Melissa and Will reached Salt Lake City on October 6. They had traveled a long way since leaving their families, over two years before.

Suggested reading: Norma B. Ricketts, *Melissa's Journey with the Mormon Battalion* (Salt Lake City: Utah Printing Co., 1994).

14

# WESTERN MECCA FOR AN EASTERN GIRL

Frances (Fannie) Mullen was born and raised in New York City, and she thought it was the only habitable place on earth. But when the nineteen-year-old girl married twenty-three-year-old Lieutenant Orsemus Boyd in October, 1867, she determined to follow him as soon as he learned his new duty station, even if it was at the end of the earth.

Orsemus, from Delaware County, New York, had joined the New York Volunteers for duty in the Civil War when he was sixteen. He was soon promoted to second lieutenant, and was probably the only officer in the Union Army with both his brother and his father as enlisted men under his command. After two years service, he was appointed to West Point in 1863, graduating in 1867.

Orsemus was assigned to the 8th Cavalry, which was scattered over the West. When he left New York three days after their wedding, he told Fannie he would send for her as soon as he could.

The following January, Fannie boarded a steamer for Panama. Orsemus knew by then that he was going to a remote area in Nevada, and he thought Fannie could at least come as far as San Francisco. Fannie enjoyed the balmy weather as she crossed Panama and boarded another steamer for San Francisco.

When she reached San Francisco, Fannie learned that Orsemus was stationed at Fort Halleck in northeastern Nevada, where the 8th Cavalry protected railroad builders from hostile Indians. Seeing no reason to stay in San Francisco, she took another steamer to Sacramento and bought railroad passage to Cisco, the end of the railroad being built eastward over the Sierras.

She left Cisco at noon in a heavy snowstorm. She and one other passenger—also a woman—traveling by sleigh and stage, did not reach Virginia City until ten the next morning.

The sleigh ride was pleasant. They had warm blankets and robes, and the slow travel through the massive, scenic mountains was enjoyable. But when the storm ended and they changed to a stagecoach, Fannie realized that stages were meant to be used by a coach full of passengers who could keep their seats under all conditions. She and her sole travel companion tried to brace themselves in the lurching, bouncing vehicle, and finally had to lie face down on the floor to keep the bruising to a minimum.

How things changed in Virginia City! Now the stage was jammed full. When Fannie or her companion—sitting side by side on the rear seat and facing the men sitting across from them on the middle seat—wanted to move their feet, the other passengers were required to move theirs at the same time. The men sympathized with the women, and suggested that they would fold blankets across their laps and the ladies could bend forward, lay their heads on the blankets, and get some well deserved rest. The women tried it, but could not sleep in the awkward position.

Fannie had enjoyed looking up at high rocky precipices and down into tree-filled canyons in California, but she dd not think much of Nevada scenery. There were no trees, only sagebrush and greasewood. Fannie thought the rivers hardly deserved the name, especially when, at Austin, she saw that the Reese River could be crossed with one step.

It took five days and nights of sleepless travel to reach Camp Ruby, a military outpost at the southern end of the Ruby Mountains. Fannie was so excited to meet Orsemus, who had come down from Fort Halleck with an ambulance, that she hardly remembered to say goodbye to her friend who continued on eastward with the stage.

Fannie was exhausted, and Orsemus waited two days before they left Camp Ruby in a government ambulance. They still had four days of travel to reach his duty station, over a hundred miles to the north.

The ambulance Orsemus brought did not have the usual cross seats. It had narrow seats down each side, which could be slid together to form a bed. During the day, Fannie's trunk and the hay piled on top took up so much room behind the driver that Fannie and Orsemus could barely squeeze in at the rear. At night the trunk and hay were put outside, and they expected to sleep comfortably, as they had plenty of blankets.

Fannie had never camped out before, and her first night was memorable. They had to tie each of their four mules to a wheel on the ambulance, as the sagebrush was too small to furnish secure ties. Shortly after falling asleep, Fannie was jolted awake when the ambulance lurched and pitched, almost upsetting. They discovered that one mule had slid under the vehicle in its sleep and had tried to stand up too quickly. Orsemus assured Fannie they'd have four walls around them the next two nights.

But the four walls enclosed a cabin just eighteen feet square with ten other men in it. The small bed in the corner was only a rude, pine bunk, but it was better than the mud floor, so Fannie accepted with thanks. The men, to show their hospitality, even draped rough curtains around the bed.

The next night's cabin was about the same size, but it had fifteen men in it. Again Fannie and Orsemus enjoyed the hospitality typical of men who seldom saw women, but who remembered their mothers and sisters.

A snowstorm blew up during the night. When Fannie woke and looked through the curtains around their bed she saw that six dogs had crept inside to lie asleep among their fifteen hosts.

Ten inches of snow fell during the night, and their ambulance got stuck the next morning in a deep drift. The men at the cabin sent their open, springless wagon to bring the travelers back. They were only eighteen miles from the fort, and Fannie persuaded the men to let them go on. Snow fell hard all day, and it took twelve hours to reach the fort. It was not until this, the last day of a long trip, that Fannie let down her guard. She was crying when Orsemus lifted her out of the wagon and carried her into the tent that would be her home for the next year.

Actually, Fannie's new home consisted of two tents, each one eight feet square. A calico curtain divided the sitting room from the bedroom. Barley sacks carpeted the floors. She appreciated her new quarters more when she learned that enlisted men did not even have tents. They lived in dugouts—mere holes in the ground—which, while warm enough, to Fannie's mind were suitable only for animals.

Fannie knew little about riding but she learned on a steady old horse called Honest John. By spring she could ride anywhere.

The gnats, the wasps, and the glaring summer sun which penetrated their tents to burn Fannie's skin were as exasperating as the bitter winter cold. But she wrote about "lovely wild flowers, a ceaseless delight, and our camp on a lovely little stream in a grove of cottonwood trees," which was for her more beautiful than she could ever have imagined.

During their second winter in the tents, Orsemus was promoted to first lieutenant and transferred to another company of the regiment in Prescott, Arizona. The transfer came at a good time, as their daughter was born in San Francisco while they were waiting for transportation. On the baby's three-week birthday they left a steamer in Wilmington to begin a long, hot wagon ride to Prescott.

With the annual increase in Orsemus' pay of one hundred dollars, Fannie hired a servant. Failing to find a woman who would go to Arizona, she hired a twelve-year-old Chinese boy, the first of his race to enter Arizona territory.

It took ten days to travel to Fort Mohave at the Colorado River, four more to reach Prescott. Fannie liked Prescott. She wrote: "Everything seemed delightful. Situated among the hills, surrounded by trees and with a most enjoyable climate, but bracing at all seasons, it would indeed prove a desirable home to wanderers like ourselves, and I fondly hoped we might remain there."

But Orsemus' company was transferred to Camp Date Creek, sixty miles southwest, "a desolate and undesirable locality. The only pretty spot was a slow, sluggish stream some miles away, where no one dared remain long for fear of malaria."

As the only woman within fifty miles, Fannie learned to provide hospitality to travelers—both army and stage riders—passing through the barren country. She also learned to live with centipedes, scorpions, and rattlesnakes, which were attracted to their mud-brick (adobe) shelter. But she remembered her year in Arizona as a happy one with many visitors. She had killed so many rattlesnakes that she had a box full of rattles by the time the regiment was moved to New Mexico.

Camp Date Creek had become Fannie's first real home. In spite of its desolation, it seemed to her on leaving to be "the most delightful imaginable spot." She cried bitterly for days. As they traveled south to Tucson and then east to Camp Bowie, native women would gather around in the evening to watch with wonder as Fannie bathed her little girl. Apaches used water only for drinking.

After crossing the pass near Cooke's Peak —the scene of more Indian attacks than any other place in Apache country—they reached Fort Selden on the Rio Grande, crossed the White Sands, and moved on to Fort Stanton in the pine forests of Lincoln County, New Mexico Territory. There they lived a happy, peaceful year in a two-room stone house with detached kitchen and dining room. Fannie enjoyed trout fishing in mountains of spectacular beauty.

In March, 1871, Fanny decided to return to New York City for a visit and to recover her health. Orsemus rode with her to Denver, five hundred miles away, where they spent a week together before Fannie took the train east. As she approached "dingy St. Louis, her heart sank at the prospect of breathing air so heavy and dense that it suffocated," and she fondly recalled Denver's sweet, pure air.

Finally she reached the city of her youth and stood in front of the Fifth Avenue Hotel, her most familiar landmark. She had seen it built, had always lived nearby, and passed it daily on the way to school. When lonely in her army life, thinking of the hotel had brought the happiest feelings. But seeing it now made her heart sick with loneliness for her western home.

After three months, she went to the Catskills where her husband had grown up. The mountains seemed insipid after the rocky grandeur of the West, but she had to stay until her son was born and her husband came for a long visit.

They took the train back to Cheyenne, where Fannie and the children waited for Orsemus to go to Fort Stanton and return with an army ambulance for his family. It was May, 1872, and the trip back to her home in New Mexico Territory was pure pleasure. "Every whiff of mountain air was inhaled with delight, for, like a Mohammedan, my face was turned toward Mecca."

Suggested reading: Mrs. Orsemus Boyd, *Cavalry Life in Tent and Field* (Lincoln: University of Nebraska Of Press, 1982).

# ANOTHER NEW YORK WIFE

Comparing two women from New York provides an interesting picture of the variety among wives in the frontier army after the Civil War. Although Fannie Mullen Boyd passed the Fifth Avenue School every day, her writing gives the impression that her people were probably workers or tradesmen in the city. Eveline Martin's great-uncle had been governor of New York, and the girl was raised in a palatial western New York home. Her father had been the governor's private secretary, and he practiced law with William Seward, a future secretary of state. Ambassadors, cabinet officers, senators, and other dignitaries were frequent guests in the Martin home.

Evy Martin married Andrew Alexander during the Civil War. At war's end he was ordered to cavalry duty in New Mexico. A captain in the regular army, Andrew was an acting battalion commander in the Third Cavalry. The comparison between Evy's journey to join her husband with Fannie Boyd's to join hers is interesting. Fannie rode three steamships, two trains, a sleigh, a crowded stage and, finally, an army ambulance to reach her husband.

After a day spent "in the toil of packing" Evy boarded a train from her Mt. Auburn, New York, home. Her father traveled with her. They had a sleeping car overnight to Cincinnati, where they visited family friends before traveling on to Odin, Illinois, a "rather heathenish place," she thought. The servants at her tavern didn't even know where a church was. It was Sunday, and Evy, a Sunday School teacher, found a Presbyterian church where the sermon was filled with "curious western expressions." She also found a Sunday School class without a teacher and "sowed a little seed by the wayside."

Her father left her at Cairo after arranging for a stateroom on the next steamer down the Mississippi River. Evy was amused the next morning when she realized that she had loaded her little pistol and placed it under her pillow but had forgotten to lock her stateroom door.

When Evy reached Memphis early in the morning, she was met by General George Stoneman (a future governor of California on whose staff Evy's husband had served during the Civil War). He took Evy to his home, and the family entertained her until her steamer left that evening.

After a two-day, three-night steamship ride up the White River, Evy was met at DeVall's Bluff by a sergeant with a note that Andrew would meet her at Fort Smith. Evy was disappointed but "attended to" by a polite acquaintance of her husband. Here Evy met black troops for the first time. She was shocked to discover that their officers were "more low and uneducated than I had supposed them." In fact, all officers of black troops at that time were white, among them some of the most distinguished officers in the army.

A major met Evy at Little Rock and took her to his home, where he and his wife welcomed her and entertained her for four days. Then a colonel took her to the next steamer, where she received a send off serenade by a regimental band.

Andrew met Evy in Fort Smith and they lived in a tent for a few days. She didn't have to worry about sunburn in her tent. It was "lined with blue army blankets, which not only protect it from dampness and make it much cooler on hot days, but subdue the light, which makes a distressing glare in the canvas tents. I have a buffalo skin for a carpet, and my bed is covered with the red blanket Fanny Rawles (a colonel's wife) gave me."

The regiment had a review before starting for New Mexico. Evy accepted the colonel's invitation to ride at his side, although she declined his offer to receive the regimental salute as the reviewing officer. Her account gives a much different picture of equestrian skill than Fannie Boyd's account of learning on old Honest John.

"I rode Zaidee (the first time since Knoxville) and wore my grey riding habit and black velvet hat. Zaidee behaved beautifully. After the regiment had passed in review before the colonel, we rode along the line and, as the ground was rough and full of ditches, Zay distinguished herself. The first ditch we came to was rather wide, but she took it like a bird and behaved throughout with the most perfect decorum. Zaidee was very much complimented on her behavior and appearance."

It was late May, but Andrew kept a kettle full of coals from the company kitchen in the door of their tent on rainy days to keep her comfortable.

Evy was very disturbed by the profanity of the troops. She heard Andrew tell some buglers that he would cut them over the head with his saber if he caught them swearing around his tent. He kept his saber hanging at the door to remind them.

Evy described some of the women in the regiment as "a rather queer set. Mrs. C was a company washerwoman before her husband was promoted from the ranks. Mrs. K and her daughter are very common. Mrs. H and Patrita are Mexicans."

Fannie Boyd never mentioned riding with the regiment. Evy's description as they started on the march to New Mexico is colorful.

She led the order of march for Andrew's battalion in an ambulance, followed by a soldier leading Zaidee, saddled and bridled and with a waterproof covering over the saddle. Then followed Andrew and the other officers, followed by their companies, their guidons flying. The company ambulances and wagons followed and the beef herd brought up the rear.

Evy admitted that she "presented quite a funny appearance." She was seated in a high rocking chair which was fastened by cleats to the bottom of the ambulance. Under her chair were her tin washbowl and pitcher. Two leather pockets in front held her revolver and field glasses. After a few hours, she took pity on a dog with puppies and let them ride in the ambulance with her.

Three days into the journey, Evy described her costume for crossing the plains (present Oklahoma and the Texas panhandle). Riding at the head of the column with Andrew, she wore a black and white traveling dress with a large flat hat that had a blue veil hanging from the edge. She wore a miniature pistol belt with a little pistol on one side and a silver-hilted dagger which a colonel had given her on the other.

When they reached Fort Bascom she called on the commander's wife, as etiquette required. She found her an "exceedingly ugly Mexican lady." Evy did add that she thought Mexicans made good troops as long as they were officered by white men.

On reaching Fort Union, Andrew was assigned to build a new fort in Colorado Territory. While there Evy became a close friend of Kit Carson. She also wrote about spending a long afternoon in a tete-a-tete with William Sherman, Chief General of the Army. While at the new station, she got her first mail in a month and learned from her sisters that the family had recently entertained President Johnson, General Grant, and Admiral Farragut at the family home.

Evy repeatedly called black troops darkies, and she displayed racial prejudice against Mexicans and Indians. But she also helped organize quick defenses in an unexpected attack by Indians.

Interestingly, when Andrew was promoted to major he was assigned to the 9th Cavalry, a black regiment. Evy's diary ends before Andrew joined the new regiment, but we know that he fit right in with other distinguished officers of one of the army's best cavalry regiments.

Eveline Martin Alexander and Fannie Mullen Boyd, so different in many ways, each was married to an outstanding officer and each supported that officer very well. Living in a country of diversity, each rendered good service to that country as an army wife.

Suggested reading: Sandra L. Myres (Ed.) *Cavalry Wife, the Diary of Eveline M. Alexander* (College Station: Texas A&M University Press, 1977).

# ARMY WIFE, ARMY MOTHER

In the early 1840s Catharine Wever left Weverton, Maryland—named for her father—and journeyed by rail, steamer, and stage to Hillsboro, Ohio, to visit her sister, a doctor's wife. Catharine's father, Caspar Wever, was a noted engineer and superintendent of construction for the Baltimore and Ohio Railroad.

In Hillsboro, Catharine met a lawyer, William Collins, and in 1843 they were married in Weverton. Catharine, twenty-five, was nine years younger than her husband. He had been married back in his native Connecticut, but when his young wife died—about eight years before he met Catharine—he moved west to Ohio.

Catharine's and William's first child and only son was born in November, 1844. They named him Caspar after Catharine's father. They later had two daughters, Mary who died at age six and Josephine who grew to adulthood but was an invalid for much of her life.

When William and his new bride reached Hillsboro, they started construction on property he owned north of the town. A year later they moved into a stately Colonial home, naming it Dogwood Knob after the beautiful trees that grew on the property. It became the center for gracious hospitality among the citizens of Hillsboro.

Catharine was trained in art and she helped Caspar become a skilled artist. He also loved books, his sisters, and the endless pranks the merry, imaginative boy thought up. Catharine was also a fine gardener and her extensive gardens enhanced the beauty of the family home.

In 1849 William became the president of a local railroad company. In 1861 he raised a regiment of volunteer cavalry for service in the Civil War. The next spring, with seventeen-year-old Caspar marching with them, the regiment was sent to Wyoming to relieve another cavalry regiment. Catharine was anxious about her only son—too young to enlist—going off to fight Indians. William took a reduction in rank to lieutenant colonel so he could lead one of the battalions in the field.

Colonel Collins' men idolized him. One soldier wrote: "He was a fine old gentleman, rather old for military service (he was fifty-three) but finely preserved, energetic, and soldierly."

Caspar had been his father's companion on many hunting and fishing trips, but he was not a robust young man, and he had a persistent cough when he left home. On the long march west he lost his cough, gained a deep tan, and seemed to grow quickly into a man. One soldier wrote that Caspar "was apparently a young man entirely devoid of fear and with an ambition to have military success and renown."

Catharine Collins was a Sunday School teacher, and she belonged to literary clubs. But when the Civil War started she joined her sister in Sanitary Committee work (predecessor of the Red Cross) and made that work her priority.

Colonel Collins asked Catharine to join him at Fort Laramie in Fall, 1863. She traveled by steamboat, railroad, stage, and ambulance to reach the fort in November. By that time eighteen-year-old Caspar had enlisted and was soon commissioned a second lieutenant.

Most of Catharine's letters to Josephine were about the girl's behavior, keeping up with her music training, and the need to improve her penmanship, accuracy, and style in writing. Not much was said about Catharine's experience at Fort Laramie, although it was much different than that of wives of junior officers at less developed posts.

Catharine mentioned several times that her husband was working too hard and suffering from mountain fever, colic, and facial pain. Most of Caspar's assignments during the nine months his mother was at Laramie were at forts further west, but her few remarks showed much motherly pride.

Two weeks after Catharine's arrival at the fort, the wife of the telegraph operator had a little girl, and Catherine went there every morning to wash and dress the baby. Then her husband took sick, and she cared for him. She also visited soldiers in the post hospital.

When a soldier was killed by a falling adobe wall, Catharine comforted the widow and her five children. They had come from Kansas just six weeks before. She also attended the burial with its full military honors in place of her husband who was sick.

Catharine described Company D's Christmas dinner, to which all the battalion wives were invited. They had roast pig, roast beef, and cold-boiled ham, jellies, pickles, coffee, tea, peaches, cake, mince pie, and ice cream. Catharine had no idea where they got all the tablecloths and dishes. The post sutler invited her to a cake and egg-nog party that evening. She accepted on condition that she could pass up the egg-nog. Catharine was an active member of the Hillsboro Crusade, sometimes called the Whirlwind of the Lord, which spread to become the Woman's Christian Temperance Union.

The name of William Collins' horse was Honest John. Though "gay and fast, the horse was not difficult to manage." The horse is not mentioned again in the Collins letters, but the name brings up an interesting speculation. Four years later, Fannie Boyd, married to a lieutenant in the 8th Cavalry and stationed at Fort Halleck in Nevada, described how she learned to ride on Honest John, a "steady old horse." Fort Laramie and Fort Halleck were both on the emigrant trail to California. It makes one wonder if Honest John traveled with Indians or emigrants or both down the trail to the west. How

CATHARINE WEVER COLLINS

American Heritage Center, University of Wyoming

the people in Nevada would know his name is no more intriguing a question than how two horses would have the same unusual name.

The growing trouble with Indians led to Catharine's return to Ohio in 1864. She left Fort Laramie on August 4, traveling with one other woman in army ambulances and with an escort. When they reached Julesburg they learned that the night before, Indians had killed thirty-one emigrants in what is called the Plum Creek Massacre. They would have to pass this point several days ahead.

The women were traveling with General Robert B. Mitchell, commander of the District of the Platte. At three o'clock the morning they reached Julesburg, General Mitchell had dismissed their escort to return to Fort Laramie. After telegraphing ahead, the general decided to go on. Apparently they just had two ambulances with their drivers. He told the women that if they were attacked, he would corral the wagons and the women were to lie flat on the ground, hoping all bullets and arrows would pass over their heads.

Two days later, two very anxious women (and perhaps a couple of anxious soldiers) met two companies moving west to Julesburg. Twenty men were detailed to turn around and escort the general's party back to Fort Kearney. They arrived at the fort without difficulty, but most of the stages were not running, and the few that were could barely hold the frightened passengers that squeezed aboard. Catharine and the other woman traveler, along with eleven other passengers, rode a stage to Omaha, arriving at two o'clock in the morning on August 19. They immediately boarded a steamboat which got them to St. Joseph the next day.

Catharine Collins made Hillsboro her residence until she died in 1911, aged ninety-three. She probably never really enjoyed being an army wife on the frontier and away from her beautiful home and gardens.

Caspar Collins, a very brave young man, was killed by Indians in 1865 near a small fort guarding the Platte River Bridge. The army renamed the fort Fort Caspar, and the town that grew up nearby was misspelled Casper, Wyoming.

A fort in northern Colorado and the town that grew up nearby were named after Catharine's husband, William.

Suggested reading: Agnes Wright Spring, "An Army Wife Goes West." in *The Colorado Magazine 31(4)* (October, 1954).

# TWO CARRINGTON WIVES

rances Courtney—called Miss Fanny by her many friends—lived in Franklin, Tennessee. Although her brother served in the Confederate Army, Fanny, along with sister Florence and their mother, attended wounded Union soldiers in their Presbyterian Church after the battle of Franklin in November, 1864.

Shortly after the war Florence married a Union officer from New York. Later that 1865 summer, Fanny married Lieutenant George Washington Grummond whom she met when his Michigan regiment came to Franklin. Grummond had enlisted as a sergeant and risen to lieutenant colonel, with a brevet to brigadier general. He was most proud, however, of his new commission as a second lieutenant in the regular army.

After service on Governor's Island in New York harbor and at Vicksburg, Grummond was posted to Fort Phil Kearny in present Wyoming. Fanny was glad to leave the Mississippi heat after the hot summer of 1866. They traveled by steamboat to Omaha and by train to the end of the railroad. Fanny was the only woman on the first passenger train to travel that far west of Omaha.

They continued by ambulance, sometimes sleeping at ranches, sometimes under the stars. Fanny, pregnant, clapped her hands with joy when, on September 17, she first saw the fort that would be her new home. She called it "a place of refuge from fatigue and danger," more meaningful, even, than "the shadow of a rock in a weary land."

However, their small detail had to wait at the gate to allow entry of a wagon carrying a recently-killed and scalped soldier. He had been killed a short time before as Indians attacked a group of men cutting wood a short distance west. Frances was appalled at her introduction to the Indian Wars.

Fort Phil Kearny was one of three forts built and garrisoned by the 18th Infantry, commanded by Colonel Henry B. Carrington. A Yale graduate, Carrington had organized the Ohio militia in the Civil War, and he later received a colonel's commission in the regular army. A scholarly man, Carrington had been a desk officer throughout the war; he had no combat experience.

At first, the Grummonds had no personal quarters. Two tents were erected for them, and Fanny kept her trunks, two camp stools, and a mess chest in the front tent. She and her husband occupied the rear tent with its two hospital bunks and a small stove. The cook stove was behind the tent under a tarpaulin. It snowed the first night at the fort—Fanny's first night in a tent—but the Grummonds felt safe and warm. By morning the snow was deep, some drifting in to fall on Fanny's face.

The three companies garrisoning the fort had their own band. On Sundays they played hymns, sometimes adding *Annie Laurie* and *When the Swallows Homeward Fly*. They had no chapel but used the newest building available at the time for worship.

Fanny soon learned from Carrington's wife, Margaret, about the Indian problem. The fort, with Fort Reno to the south and Fort C. F. Smith to the north were built to protect gold hunters and other travelers on the Bozeman Trail. But the trail crossed a hundred twenty-five thousand square miles of the last and best hunting grounds of the Indians. Their rights to the land had been confirmed in the Fort Laramie Treaty in 1851 and renewed in another treaty just one year before Fannie and Grummond arrived.

Colonel and Margaret Carrington soon moved into their half-completed quarters, and Frances and her husband took over the large hospital tent that the Carringtons had been using. Three weeks later, they moved into a brand new pine-log house with three rooms. Fanny made window shades from newspapers, and the company tailor sewed gunny sacks into carpeting. Fanny paid seventy-five cents a pound for "salty and rather ancient butter." She found she could make it more edible by working hot water into it.

On October 30 the flagstaff was completed with a bandstand at its base. Speaking at the dedication ceremony, Carrington reminded the small garrison of three hundred and fifty—including the wood cutters, scouts , and five officer's wives—that in the fifteen weeks of construction, one officer and seven enlisted had already been killed, in addition to several civilians.

Early in December a lieutenant was promoted to captain, and he and his family were transferred to Omaha for a new assignment. Fanny and her husband received some crockery and a small milk cow from the transferred officer. She hired a soldier to do the milking.

Grummond did not have to wait long for action. On December 6 he volunteered to lead the mounted infantry in an attack against Indians. Only the speed of his horse saved him from ambush. Another lieutenant and a sergeant were killed. The lieutenant was a Mason, and Grummond, also a member, conducted the burial rites.

On December 21, Grummond got his second chance. The wood cutters had been attacked by a small band of warriors. Captain William Fetterman led a rescue party, composed of fifty infantry and thirty mounted men. Again, Grummond commanded the mounted troops. He was the only married man in the rescue party. Fanny, remembering the hairbreadth escape only two weeks before, dreaded to see him go.

The soldiers saw ten young warriors taunting them as they rode out of the fort. The warriors waved blankets and shouted insults, inviting the soldiers to pursue. What the soldiers did not see was a hidden force of

FRANCES GRUMMOND CARRINGTON

American Heritage Center, University of Wyoming

fifteen hundred warriors, waiting for the decoy to work.

The trap was sprung, and this time no one returned. A relief party was able to recover forty-nine bodies, but no one knew that night what had happened to the rest, including Grummond.

Everyone at the fort loved Fanny. Margaret Carrington praised her "Christian fortitude" as Fannie spent that dreadful night of fear and uncertainty, not knowing whether her husband was already dead or being tortured to death.

John, (Portugee) Phillips, a civilian scout who lived at the fort with his wife and two children, answered Carrington's call for a volunteer to ride two hundred thirty-five miles to Fort Laramie for help. He came to Fanny's quarters with tears in his eyes.

"I'm going to Laramie for help," he said, "even if it costs me my life. I'm going for your sake. Here is my wolf robe. I brought it to you to keep and remember me by if you never see me again."

Colonel Carrington himself unlocked the sally port gate and let Phillips out, mounted on one of the colonel's thoroughbreds. It was forty below zero, one of the coldest nights of the winter. Phillips reached Fort Laramie on Christmas night, and his borrowed horse fell dead from exhaustion as soon as they were inside the walls of the fort.

After a night of horror but no sleep, Fanny knew in her heart, as did the others, that all the missing men were dead. At least, they hoped they were dead, considering the alternative. But there was still a heated discussion about what to do. Most of the officers thought it was dangerous for those remaining in the fort to send out a recovery party. Carrington finally ended the discussion with a decision that presaged one made half a world away and almost ninety years later by Marines in frozen Korea.

"We'll not leave our men's bodies with the enemy," Carrington announced quietly.

The colonel left orders that if the Indians attacked while the soldiers were gone, all the women and children were to be put in the magazine. It was to be blown up, should the Indians succeed in capturing the fort.

The women watched through a long, long day. Fanny wrote: "Mrs. Carrington tenderly took me to her arms and to her home where in silence we awaited the unfolding of this deadly sorrow."

Margaret Carrington, herself, knew about grief. Orphaned in infancy, in the years 1852 to 1864 she lost five of her own children, none reaching the age of three.

The soldiers returned after sunset with all the bodies. Carrington would not allow Fanny to see the mutilated body of her husband. He did cut off a lock of Grummond's hair and presented that to the young widow. He also told her that the number of spent cartridges around his body showed the ferocity of the defense he and his comrades had put up.

Fanny never returned to her own quarters. From then on, her home was with Margaret Carrington. Fanny wrote that other wives "combined with Mrs. Carrington in the hasty preparation of such garments as would be in harmony with my lonely condition, and thus ward off thoughtless intrusion from whatever source." We don't know how long she was in mourning.

Six companies marched up from Fort Laramie to relieve Fort Phil Kearny. Temperatures ran from twenty-five to forty degrees below zero, and the snow was knee deep.

On January 23, in another snow storm, Fannie, the Carringtons, and other wives left the fort with an escort of sixty soldiers. Fanny had her own wagon, and another held Grummond's coffin. They traveled only six miles in their first day of eight hours.

Many amputations of frozen digits and legs were made during their three-day layover at Fort Reno. Margaret Carrington's driver died when both his legs were removed, and another man also died after his amputation.

They continued with a reduced escort to Fort Laramie. From there Fannie, with a few more wagons of travelers, went on to Fort McPherson, arriving in late February.

Fannie continued on by train, crossing the icebound Missouri River in a stagecoach. She reached her Tennessee home in March after a harrowing journey of seven weeks. She buried her husband, and, a month later, her son was born.

The Fetterman massacre—the main army disaster of the Indian Wars until the Little Bighorn Battle ten years later—ended Carrington's effective military career. Margaret died a few months before he retired in December, 1870.

When Fanny read about Margaret's death, she wrote a sympathy letter to Carrington. After more correspondence, Carrington and Fanny married on April 3, 1871. He adopted her son, and they had three more children. He encouraged Fanny to write about her experiences as an army wife, just as he had earlier encouraged Margaret. Both wrote books about their experiences.

Fanny and Carrington both attended the dedication ceremony in 1908 of a monument at the site of the fight where Lieutenant Grummond was killed. Fanny died of cancer in 1911, one year before her second husband.

Suggested reading: Frances Carrington, *My Army Life* (Boulder: Pruett Publishing Co., 1990).

## SERVICE IN THE NORTHERN ROCKIES

When the Civil War started, twenty-two-year-old Elizabeth Johnston Reynolds of Piqua, Ohio, volunteered as a nurse. She was assigned to a hospital in Cincinnati. The next January she was treating a severely wounded first lieutenant from the 18th United States Infantry. His name was Andrew (Andy) Sheridan Burt, he was eight months younger than Elizabeth, and he hadn't wasted any time becoming an officer in the regular army.

A Yale dropout, Andy Burt enlisted on the first day that President Lincoln called for volunteers. One month later he was commissioned in the 18th Infantry, commanded by Colonel Henry B. Carrington.

Andy didn't waste any time courting Elizabeth, either. They were married in September, 1863. By the time their son was born the following July, he was a captain.

Andy served with distinction in the Civil War, receiving a brevet to major for bravery in the Atlanta campaign. By war's end the 18th had suffered staggering losses in men. Recruited back to full strength, it was the first regular infantry unit sent to the Indian frontier.

The regiment was divided among several posts. Headquarters and three companies went to build Fort Phil Kearny in northern Wyoming. Other companies went to posts in Colorado, Nebraska, and Wyoming. Andy, commanding two companies, was assigned to Fort Bridger in southwestern Wyoming.

There was no bridge across the Mississippi, so Andy's companies marched across the frozen river to Jefferson Barracks at St. Louis. While they waited to go on, Elizabeth's younger sister, Kate, joined them. They marched again from Fort Leavenworth, reaching Fort Bridger on July 13, 1866. On the way they met a band of Indians who offered thirty horses to buy their two-year-old, Little Andrew. Elizabeth was horrified.

When the Burts arrived, Fort Bridger already had a twenty-four-year history as a noted fort in the West. It had been a trading fort for trappers, Indians, and emigrants, a Mormon outpost, an important military post, and a station for Pony Express, mail, telegraph and stage lines. Elizabeth probably didn't know how lucky she was until she talked to other army women about some of the places they had occupied. Tired of the sage brush, prickly pear, and greasewood in the country they had crossed, she wrote, "We looked down upon the valley and Ft. Bridger in which our new home was to be, and our hearts were filled with joy."

Their quarters were constructed of hewn logs. They had four rooms, two on each side of a large hall. "On one side were two sleeping rooms and closets; on the other was a living room, dining room, and a pantry with a small kitchen and a tiny room for Maggie (her servant) in the rear. All were plastered and looked very comfortable."

Each larger room had an open fireplace. Elizabeth put a Brussels rug in the living room and army blankets, sewn together, became rugs in the other rooms. She made curtains of pretty material she had brought, and also used it to cover packing boxes which served as toilet tables and wash stands. They had brought a few lamps, but the quartermaster had no coal oil and it was too expensive at the traders, so they used candles. The Burts, including sister Kate, enjoyed riding, hunting, and fishing in their beautiful valley.

In October Elizabeth, along with her son and sister and the trader's daughter, traveled with a lieutenant and the post surgeon to Fort Douglas at Salt Lake City to visit a major and his family. It was a three day trip in two army ambulances, and they stayed over four days. Elizabeth thought the major's quarters, near a city, were luxurious. The weather was unusually warm going to Utah, but they ran into a fierce blizzard before getting back to Fort Bridger. Their driver lost the road, and they spent the night in the ambulance, huddled under buffalo robes. They listened to the howling wind and worried about wolves.

Visibility was only two feet in the morning, so they decided to stay where they were. Later that day, they were rescued by a wood-cutting detail from the fort, who did not know they were lost.

Evenings at the fort were spent in reading, writing letters, playing whist, and exchanging visits with the trader's family. They had no chaplain or any special religious services. However Elizabeth taught what she could of the Bible and the Calvary Catechism to her own son and to six children of the soldiers.

As Christmas approached, they heard through the mail of the increasing Indian trouble at Fort Phil Kearny. The news was depressing, but for their son's sake, they tried to enter into the spirit of the season. The trader brought gifts with his ox train, and he gave young Andrew the first mechanical toy the Burts had ever seen. They hung stockings, and Elizabeth made her six Sunday School scholars happy with homemade candy, ice cream, cookies, and doughnuts.

But shortly after Christmas they began hearing rumors from the Indian underground of a great defeat at Fort Phil Kearny. They refused to believe that such a disaster could have happened to their friends in other companies of the regiment, and they were shocked when the official report arrived. Burt was transferred to the 2nd Battalion, but he didn't have to leave until the first empty wagon train came east from Salt Lake. Elizabeth, relieved, thought that would not happen until summer.

The wagon train came through in early June. It included a hundred ex-Mormons, returning east from Salt Lake. Elizabeth was expecting, and this may have had something to do with Burt's change of orders. He was to stop in Fort Sanders for temporary duty and then go on to Omaha to bring out new recruits for the 27th Infantry. His new regiment, created out of the Second Battalion of the 18th, would be stationed at Fort C. F. Smith, in Montana Territory.

They reached Fort Sanders on July 3. Expecting a baby soon, Elizabeth arranged with an ex-Mormon family to hire their twelve-year-old girl. The family was large, and the parents were glad to spare Christina on condition that Elizabeth teach her domestic skills.

When the new baby, Edith, was three weeks old, Burt went on to Omaha. The quartermaster had fixed up temporary quarters for the family in the fort's blockhouse. Burt, as well as other officers recommended that Elizabeth go back to Ohio with her sister and the children as soon as her health permitted. But she did not want to leave Andy, so she arranged to meet him at Fort D. A. Russell on his way back with the recruits. They left Fort Sanders in the middle of October in a snowstorm.

As Elizabeth was leaving Fort Russell to meet Andy at his camp on Lodge Pole Creek, Colonel John Gibbon handed her a bottle of gin, saying it was for the baby when she had colic. Elizabeth said she had never used gin.

"Then you don't know what a blessing it will prove," the colonel said. "I have raised a large family out here in the West, and I know."

Maggie the servant girl was reluctant to go past Fort Fetterman, saying there were too many Indians. She didn't have much choice. At that fort the post commander lived in a dugout cut into a river bank.

When they reached the Crazy Woman Fork on November 13, they were attacked by Indians trying to steal their mules. Elizabeth, Kate, Christina, and the baby lay as flat on the bottom of their wagon as they could while bullets whistled overhead. Elizabeth worried about their son, as he was staying in a tent with his father. No one was hurt.

They spent three days at Fort Phil Kearny, the scene eleven months earlier of the Fetterman disaster. Going on toward their new post, they met a band of friendly Crow Indians. The women made a fuss over Elizabeth's baby. She allowed the one with the cleanest dress to hold the child.

Three months earlier, Fort C. F. Smith had been the scene of one of the most courageous fights in the Indian Wars. Nineteen soldiers and twelve civilians, fighting in the open against about five hundred Cheyenne Indians, held out for four hours until relieved. Nevertheless, because of its remote location away from roads and trails, the fort was—and its location still is— one of the least known in the west.

The Burt's new quarters were two small rooms with dirt floors covered by gunny sacks. Elizabeth thought the two rooms would be very cozy against blizzards with three adults, Christina, and two children in them. Two Crow Indians provided once-a-month mail service between the fort and Fort Phil Kearny. Discussing the news—often quite stale—with friends helped pass many pleasant evenings.

On April 16, 1868, Elizabeth, with Kate, another woman, and three-year-old Andrew, were outside the fort picking flowers when Indians tried to stampede the fort's mule herd. Elizabeth wrote: "My sister and I each grabbed a hand of the boy and, gathering up our skirts, ran as I believe no women ever ran before."

Later in the spring the Army decided to abandon all three of their Bozeman Trail forts. The Crows who had been so friendly stole all they could as the last wagon train pulled out of the fort on July 29. As they passed through Forts Phil Kearny and Reno, the garrisons there joined them in their retreat. They "bade farewell to the land of grass and trees, trout streams and glorious mountain views."

At Fort Fetterman the Burts sold their little cow, Susie, to another officer. She had been their faithful companion for two and a half years. At Fort Russell, the regiment was transferred to posts along the railroad then under construction. Andy went to Ogallala, Nebraska Territory, but Elizabeth and the children went on to Cincinnati for a seven-month visit. She mentioned how "lovely it was to be again in the land of civilization among churches, theaters, school, fine music, meeting charming people, hearing talented men lecture, listening to the grand pipe organs, and last but not least, having access to well supplied markets."

Andy served two more years at Fort Russell, two at Fort Sanders, and two at Fort Laramie, where their third child, Reynolds Johnston Burt, was born. He and Elizabeth also served at posts in California and Arizona Territory, and again in Montana.

Andy became the best rifle shot in the army and the only officer who regularly played on baseball teams with his enlisted men. He was a retired general when he died in 1915. Elizabeth survived him by eleven years. Their youngest son also became a general.

Suggested reading: Merrill J. Mattes, *Indians, Infants, and Infantry* (Lincoln: University of Nebraska Press, 1988).

# MISSION ACCOMPLISHED, MY WORK DONE

**M**ary McGowan, born in Ireland about 1830, lost her mother when she was one year old. Her father remarried, and Mary and her older sister escaped their cruel stepmother when the sister married and took Mary with her. The three of them emigrated to St. Louis in about 1850. So far as we know, the only relatives Mary ever saw after her sister and husband died in 1857 and 1858 were the six sons she brought into the world with her soldier husband, Frank Clarke.

Frank, an Episcopal clergyman's son, emigrated from England to Wisconsin in 1847. Well educated, Frank was studying law with a firm of solicitors when he suddenly succumbed to the "American Fever" then sweeping Europe. After two years of disappointment in finding a good living, he joined the 1$^{st}$ U. S. Dragoons—forerunner of the cavalry—in 1849. He met Mary, a servant employed at Jefferson Barracks in St. Louis, and they married in December, 1850. Frank was twenty-three and Mary about three years younger.

Most of the information we have about Mary comes from her letters to Frank's mother after Frank died in the Civil War. They show an army wife in the Old West with no relatives, struggling against formidable odds to raise her sons and give them schooling she never had.

When Frank wrote to his father about Mary, Frank said, "She is a good religious honest girl. I do not say that she has the accomplishments of many of the ladies of England, but she has a good plain education and is able and willing to work, which is a great deal better out west here." Later he wrote, "on the 28$^{th}$ of December last I was married with the consent and approbation of the Colonel, and I have not from that time to the present (February 14, 1851) had the least reason to regret my choice. My wife is a clever, and I believe a truly pious girl, possessed of every qualification to make an excellent wife and me extremely happy. Her character and behaviour, whilst single, was above criticism and it is my whole study to make her comfortable, happy, and contented with her new station in life."

Mary's sister came to Fort Leavenworth, Kansas, when Charles was born the following November. By then Frank had been promoted to sergeant major, the army's highest enlisted rank.

After transfers to Fort Union in New Mexico Territory and Fort Massachusetts in what is now Colorado, Frank was at Cantonment Burgwin near Taos when their second son was born. They had named their first child after Frank's father, and they asked his parents for suggestions on naming the second. He was named Alexander after Frank's brother.

Frank had completed his five year enlistment and taken civilian employment with the army at Fort Leavenworth when their third son was born. Frank was away in the field at the time, and their first son had died after a short illness. Poor Mary delivered the third baby on September 26, 1855, the day her first son was buried. She named the new baby, Charles John, their second Charles.

Richard was born in February, 1857, the month after Frank's father died in England. John Percival followed in October, 1858. By then Mary's only relatives in the United States were her growing family of sons. She never had a daughter.

The last child, James, was born in January, 1861. By then Frank had resigned his position with the army and had bought a 174 acre farm a half mile from the garrison at Fort Riley. He also bought a bridge over the Republican River. He expected to profit from traffic to the Pike's Peak gold fields.

Frank's crops had failed from drouth in 1860, and flood waters swept his new bridge away the next spring. Then Frank bought the ferry crossing the Republican River that connected Fort Riley with Junction City.

In October, 1861, Frank was commissioned a captain in the Kansas Mounted Volunteers. In December, General James W. Denver, former Territorial Governor of Kansas, appointed Frank to his staff as assistant adjutant general. Frank and General Denver took an instant liking to each other and became close friends.

When Frank left to fight in the Civil War, Mary and the boys moved into government housing at Fort Riley. With Frank gone, she took over the task of writing to Frank's mother. Her first letter—in January, 1862—contained these sentiments:

"dear mother i feel so lonesome since he has left that i often think i would go creazy were it not for the dear children. they are such company to me. it passes a great deal of time their innocent play. dear Mother i am glad that you have quite recovered from your long and painful illness and also that you had such kind good nurses as dear sister Caroline and Agusta.

"our blessed saviour will reward them for their kindness to you. Dear Mother i will send you a copy of a letter that Governor Robinson and General Denver has sent on to Washington in order to get my dear husband a suitable commission in the regular army, as he would prefer that to being in the volunteers. It will give you an idea of what they think about him here.

"if he can spare time to write, you will no doubt have a more satisfactory letter from himself than i am capable of sending you; and when you write if you will direct to fort riley, he intends to leave me and the dear children here at least for some time yet.

"if it would not be asking you for two much we would all appreciate it very much if you will send us that likeness of yourself and our dear sisters,

36

*The Clarkes*

*Left to right,* Charles, James, Richard, Mary, John, and Alexander.

and if sister caroline will write to me sometimes i will think it a favour.

"the children joins me in kind love to yourself and their dear aunts, whom they seem to be already acquainted with. god bless you all.

Mary rented the farm for a year and hired a man to run the ferry. Frank had sold all the livestock except three cows, needed to keep the family in milk and butter. By August she had paid off the balance on a new boat for the ferry and had saved four hundred dollars.

She had also improved the punctuation in her letters to Frank's mother: "I am manageing everything the best I know how, spending as little as I can and yet it seems to take a good deal to pay the expenses of housekeeping from one month to another. in my last letter i gave you a little history of myself with regard to my friends in this and the old country, also I am, I may say, entirely alone now.

"my Dear Husband is my only friend in this country. how I do wish that this unfortunate war would cease. it will be a great blessing if we have no foreign intervention."

On December 15, 1862, Mary received a letter from Frank dated ten days earlier saying he was ill with scarlet fever and diptheria and asking her to come to Memphis to see him. She left four of the children with a neighbor and left immediately, taking seven-year-old Charles for company. She reached Memphis nine days later and learned that Frank had died twelve days before. It was a Christmas Eve she would never forget.

The army had preserved Frank's body in a vault. Mary brought it back to Fort Riley where it was buried with full military honors. She had to pay all the expenses of her travel and transporting Frank's body. She ordered a gravestone from St. Louis. The inscription ended, "he is gone and the wail of a broken hearted mourner attests too truly the loss she has sustained in this afflictive bereavement. by his beloved wife."

Mary continued to operate the ferry, but by June the river was so low she had little business. Her tenant left the farm, stealing her share of the crops, and she couldn't find another trustworthy enough to take it over.

Widows had no rights to housing on army posts. Through the kindness of the post commander and the quartermaster, she stayed until they were transferred to new assignments. However she was "ranked out" once when an officer came in with a higher rank than Frank had, and she had to move to different quarters. Also, the fort did not have an officers' mess, so Mary and the other wives had to take in boarders so the single men would have a place to eat. The extra work was a burden for her.

Mary and the boys were finally ordered out of the fort in 1865. She bought a two-room house in Junction City and enlarged it. With extra lots, it cost four thousand dollars, but she thought real estate was a good investment as the railroad was building west toward the town. In fact, the boom fizzled out when railroad construction continued west. By then Mary was receiving a widow's pension of twenty dollars a month.

By 1868 all the boys were in school, and Alexander and Charles were getting piano lessons. Charles, the best student in the school, said he wanted to study at least five different languages, including French, German, and Latin. Mary traded one of her lots for a twenty-two volume encyclopedia.

In April Mary sent her mother-in-law the book, *Life of Kit Carson*. It had been a gift to Frank ten years before, and it contained much information about places they had been and persons they had known.

Tragedy struck again in October, 1869, when ten-year-old John, playing with a shotgun, accidentally shot his brother James in the face. For three weeks, night and day, Mary applied ice packs to the boy's face. Finally his fever broke and Mary wrote: "I hope that he is entirely recovered now, but only the shadow of himself. how it makes my heart ache to look at him." The boy was blinded in one eye, but later surgeries in the hospital at Leavenworth improved his appearance.

In January, 1870, Mary started Alexander, sixteen, and Charles, fifteen, at a private school, St. Mary's College, a Jesuit elementary and secondary school which was part of the mission to the Potawatomi Indians. Three months later she entered Richard and John.

With four boys away at school and continually concerned about income, Mary rented her spacious house. When the tenant asked for a reduction in rent, she proposed to reduce it ten dollars a month provided the tenant let her have the parlor back with cooking privileges. That was satisfactory for both sides.

In May, 1870, Mary wrote her mother-in-law about how much Charles resembled his father:

"Many a bitter and sad tear have I shed with no one near me to offer me a kind or a consoling word, and sometimes by chance that the dear children would happen to see me, poor things would ask me if I was sick or what was I crying for. how little they realised what happened to them. oh when the past comes before me I feel as if my heart would bust. God forgive me if I am wrong but I cannot help it. Charles looks so like his dear father and growing more like him every day that it makes me nervous to look at him for it would seem as if it was his dear Father I was looking at when I look at him. and oh how fervently I pray morning and evening for him and the rest of them that they may walk in the path of virtue, to keep Gods commandments into his holy keeping. I offer them day and daily if I can bring them up to love and fear God in this world that they may be happy in the next, I will feel as if my mission was accomplished — My work was done."

Charles, never a robust child although a scholarly one, had to drop out of school for a year in 1871. By this time the two youngest were taking turns going to St. Mary's. Apparently their plucky Irish mother never even considered asking a child to drop out of school to help support the family, as was done so often in the Old West.

Tragedy had one final blow. The correspondence stopped abruptly when the mother-in-law died in 1872. We don't know much about Mary and her sons after that, but we do know that Charles died in 1877 after falling from a horse. He had been the best student at St. Mary's and had graduated from the University of St. Louis (probably Washington University in St. Louis). He had returned to Junction City to study law and had already been elected police judge at the time of his death.

Alexander had five children, and for many years his family lived only a few blocks from Mary.

After a lifetime of lonely struggle and triumph over adversity, Mary died in 1900, aged about seventy. No one could doubt that her mission was accomplished, her work done.

Suggested reading: Darlis A. Miller (ed.) *Above a Common Soldier* (Albuquerque: University of New Mexico Press, 1997).

# MAKING DO ON MILITARY PAY

L ouisa Hawkins grew up poor in Crawfordsville, Indiana. She would never have much money, but she brightened the lives of all who knew her. When she came home in 1837 after a visit to Kentucky, she learned that West Point Cadet Richard "Sprig" Canby was home for a short leave.

Louisa and Sprig had not paid much attention to each other before, although she knew he was religious—as she was—and had joined the temperance society before going away to college. But now the young cadet noticed the "reed-like grace of movement," the quiet voice, "rich and exquisite of tone," and the delicate manner of the girl. When he graduated two years later, he hurried home for a whirlwind courtship. Some said Louisa was too tender to be a soldier's wife. But within a month, Second Lieutenant Edward Richard Sprigg Canby was married for life to his two loves, Louisa and the United States Army.

Louisa stayed in Crawfordsville while Sprig fought in the Seminole War in Florida. He came home in 1841, sick with fever and dysentery. When the war ended the next year, he was transferred to Fort Niagara, New York. He and Louisa rented rooms nearby. Soon a daughter was born. The baby died within a few months; they never had any more children.

During the war against Mexico, Louisa stayed with an aunt in Kentucky. Then she traveled with Sprig to his next duty station in California. They lived in Monterey during the gold rush. They rented a small house, but provisions were so expensive they could not live on a captain's pay of fifty dollars a month. Sprig gardened, both for a hobby and to put food on the table; Louisa earned money working for the California Constitutional Convention, then meeting in Monterey.

Louisa was proud that her husband was liked by everyone. He was often described as a man without an enemy in his profession. Louisa, too, was universally liked for her hospitality and friendliness.

In spring 1851 Sprig was transferred to Washington, D. C., and Louisa still struggled to make ends meet on a captain's pay. Four years later Sprig was promoted to major and transferred to a new regiment formed for service on the Indian frontier. Louisa could not follow him to duty stations in Wisconsin and Minnesota, but he got a five-month leave in 1857 and spent it with her in Kentucky. Then she followed him to Fort Bridger, Wyoming.

Cooped up in tiny quarters, Louisa was overjoyed when spring finally came. She dug under the deep snowdrifts for newly-sprouting wild garlic, needed as a preventative against scurvy. A captain at the fort, writing to his wife, referred to Louisa's "amiable countenance, beaming with goodness and graciousness of heart. A truer and more amiable woman God never created, always a kind word for everyone."

Louisa lived in Santa Fe during the early Civil War, while Sprig campaigned against invading Confederates. She threw her home open to wounded soldiers from both sides, and improvised ambulances to rescue them from the battlefields. When other women protested against helping Confederates, Louisa replied: "No matter whether friend or foe; they are sons of some dear mother." Thirty years later a Texas veteran asked the Secretary of War for Louisa's address so they could invite her to their Confederate reunion.

Louisa moved to New Orleans for the last part of the Civil War, while Sprig commanded a new military division along the Mississippi. He was shot by a guerilla, and Louisa nursed him back to health.

In 1870 they moved to Portland where Sprig took command of the Department of Columbia. Living was easier on his brigadier general's pay of over three hundred dollars a month. But in April 1873 Captain Jack, a chief of the Modocs, leaped to his feet at a peace conference and shot the unarmed general dead. Canby was the highest ranking officer killed in the Indian Wars.

After her husband's body lay in state in Portland and San Francisco, Louisa accompanied it across the mountains, plains, and prairies—which he had helped secure for his country—to its burial place in Indiana.

Louisa struggled to live on the thirty dollars a month given the widows of generals. The people of Portland, learning that she was indigent, raised five thousand dollars as a gift to her. She insisted on only using the interest from the fund. When Louisa died in 1887, the five thousand dollars was returned to the city of Portland.

Suggested reading: Max L. Heyman, Jr., *Prudent Soldier* (Glendale: Arthur Clark Co., 1959).

# RIDE TO DAKOTA

In Spring, 1873, the 7th United States Cavalry, after serving in various southern states, was reunited and transferred to Dakota Territory. After riding steamers from Memphis to Cairo and trains to Yankton, ten companies mounted up for the long ride to Forts Rice and Lincoln. When Libbie Custer, wife of field commander Lt. Col. George Armstrong Custer, traced out their route almost to the British Possessions, it seemed to her as if they were going to Lapland. It was the middle of April and the troops and their wives were glad to mount up and ride into the open plains.

Libbie had heard that the climate would be "eight months of winter and four months of very late in the fall." A blizzard struck as they were organizing their mounts and wagons at Yankton and she wondered if the saying was true. The other ladies of the regiment had moved into a hotel in town, but Libbie and George took over a half-finished, two-story cabin a few miles away. It had a floor, a stairway, and a roof and little else — no stove, no chinking in the walls. The temperature dropped quickly and snow began falling as darkness approached. George was ill, and the surgeon had given Libbie medicine with the warning that she was to give it to her husband every hour.

During the first night a half dozen soldiers, lost in the storm, had seen their faint light in the window and came into the heatless shelter. More came during the night, two of them badly frozen. Libbie recognized the signs of stupor. She gave the men their only bottle of lamp alcohol and was relieved to see them revive under the fiery liquid. Then she unpacked their carpet bundles and she and her servants, Mary and Ham, rolled the stricken soldiers up in their temporary cocoons. Afterwards some had to have fingers and even feet amputated.

Day finally came, but the pale light was like twilight in the furious storm. Custer was too sick to get out of bed. Mary finally sunk down in a corner, exhausted from lack of sleep. Ham had been useless from the beginning.

Libbie scratched ice away from the coated windows and peered out. The snow reached to the top of the windows on two sides of the cabin. When night fell again and the cold increased, she believed their days were numbered.

During the second night Libbie heard the sound of mules tramping on the sheltered side of the cabin. They brayed terror as they pushed and crowded, searching for shelter. Finally they rushed away, disappearing in the great white wall of snow. All through the night a distressed horse, its wails almost human, came back at intervals. Finally Libbie pried the door open enough to look out. The strange, wild eyes of the stricken beast haunted her long afterward.

Once she heard dogs howling under the window. Realizing that they could be used as living blankets of warmth, she opened the door to let them in, but they fled into the darkness.

The groans of the soldiers from their painful and swollen feet were almost unbearable. To have shelter and be surrounded by animals appealing for help was terrible. When morning finally came, Libbie sunk into an exhausted sleep. Mary woke her with a tray of hot breakfast.

Libbie thought help had come, but Mary had cut up some large candles and pushed the small, burning ones together to heat coffee, a little meat, and a few slices of potatoes. Mary reminded Libbie how much easier it would have been had the lamp alcohol not been given away.

The snow had stopped, and Custer, feeling better, got up for breakfast. It seemed to Libbie like they were forgotten castaways, hidden under the deep drifts that surrounded them. But help did come! She heard a knock at the door and the cheery voices of Yankton citizens who had come to their relief. They had tried to come during the storm, but were unable to get through. Libbie made some excuse to go upstairs where she covered her head and tried to smother the sobs that had been suppressed during the terrors of her desolation.

Her husband found her and, after comforting her with tender words, reminded her that he would not like anyone to know that she had lost her pluck after all danger had passed.

After a ball given by Yankton citizens and a troop review staged for those citizens, the regiment headed north. Only Libbie and her sister-in-law, Margaret Custer Calhoun, were allowed to ride with the troops. The rest of the ladies of the regiment and the laundresses traveled in wagons or on the steamer that followed them along the Missouri River, carrying forage for the horses and extra supples.

Custer, his personal staff, his wife, and his sister led the march, followed by the headquarters detail. The companies, according to the order assigned for the day, followed. Whenever they reached a high bluff they enjoyed looking back at the troops, riding two abreast, followed by a long line of supply wagons. The cavalcade, winding around bends in the road and climbing over hills, was impressive.

At each evening stop Libbie would trade her riding habit for her one gown. Then while her husband read, she would sew — either a bit of needle-work or repairs to their hard-worn clothing. The soldiers who set up their tent took pride in placing their few possessions—two folding chairs, a bed, a wash-bowl with bucket and tin dipper, and a little mirror—in exactly their appointed places. Their bed consisted of two carpenter saw-horses with three boards laid on top. Sometimes Libbie and her husband strolled through the camp at twilight, and even walked among the civilian teamsters as they prepared their evening meal.

Libbie always referred to her husband as "the general," his Civil War brevet rank. He was a lieutenant colonel while in the West, except for the year he was suspended from duty without pay, a fact Libbie never mentioned. She pointed out that his thoroughbred, Dandy, was so attracted to Custer that he never was tethered. Dandy looked jealously at Custer's large band of hounds as they lay beside him, noses and paws on his chest.

When they reached Fort Sully, halfway between Yankton and their destination at Fort Lincoln, the officers and their ladies were treated to a luncheon with nine kinds of game on the table. They feasted on beaver tail, antelope, elk, buffalo tongue, wild turkey, wild goose, black-tailed deer, plover, and duck. The commanding officer's wife described her troubles with finding a governess for her children. Each new one that arrived was soon married to an officer. She wished she could find a competent governess who was old and ugly.

When they reached Fort Lincoln the regiment rode west to protect railroad surveyors and Libbie visited her family in Michigan. She would leave the fort twice more. Once was in Fall, 1874, when her husband had an extended leave of absence. They spent most of that time in New York.

The last time she left Fort Lincoln was in July, 1876. She and Margaret were the only women allowed to ride out with the regiment that spring when it rode to Montana as part of a campaign that would end at the Little Big Horn. After one night on the trail, the paymaster took the women back to the fort.

On Sunday, June 25, the day of the battle, a small group of wives at Fort Lincoln gathered to sing hymns. They hoped to relieve the anxiety that came from the brazen conduct of Indians around the fort. They wondered if the Indians knew something they didn't know. When someone suggested they sing *Nearer My God to Thee,* it was hard to force the words out over their sobs.

The terrible news arrived on July 5. Twenty-six new widows, many with children, learned the fate of most of the regiment. Libbie closed her book, "From that time the life went out of the hearts of the women who wept, and God asked them to walk on alone and in the shadow."

Libbie Custer spent the fifty-seven years of her widowhood promoting the memory of her husband. He was a splendid leader of men in battle, but it was best if someone else told him where to lead and when to fight.

Suggested reading: Elizabeth B. Custer, *Boots and Saddles* (New York: Harper & Brothers, 1885).

# A CAVALRY WIFE'S CURIOUS FOREBODING

In spring 1874, Katie Garrett visited her sister Mollie at Fort Lincoln, Dakota Territory. Mollie's husband, Donald McIntosh, was a lieutenant in Custer's 7th Cavalry. When Katie arrived, the regiment was out on a buffalo hunt, about to leave on a scout into the Black Hills.

George Custer introduced Katie to one of his lieutenants, Frank Gibson. Six years before, riding to a battle on the Washita River in Indian Territory, Gibson had described himself as one of those single men in the 7th "whose hearts were light and free and who never burdened their heads with more care than their heels could kick off."

The young lieutenant impressed Katie. She wrote:

"His campaign hat was worn at a rakish angle, and his clear, olive skin abutted in a mustache atop a mouth filled with flawless teeth. (I wonder why so many people in those old Western days had such splendid teeth. Perhaps the hardtack, tough venison, and sinewy buffalo meat had something to do with it.) The long legs of the boy lieutenant swung from his hips with the same jerky stiffness of all saddle-bound men of the plains. Impish daring danced in his large brown eyes, but it was his smile that held you with a warmth that reached out to every man, woman, child and animal alike."

That night Katie was to sleep in a tent next to the Custers' tent. She described the evening:

"The night was gorgeous, and the full moon made silvery paths through the company streets, which were barricaded at both ends against any sudden attacks from wild animals or hostiles.

"Lieutenant Gibson and I noted these things but vaguely. We were seated apart from the others and completely absorbed in the marvelous discovery of each other, while the sweet aroma from a blooming wild-rose bush nearby stole into our nostrils and combined with the magic of the moon-glow to hypnotize us into the delusion that life was just one prolonged ecstasy."

Finally, Libbie Custer had to remind Katie that it was bedtime.

The scout to the Black Hills lasted sixty days. Katie and Frank were married the day after the regiment returned to Fort Lincoln. She had been staying with her sister at that fort. As a new bride, Katie started housekeeping at Fort Rice, thirty miles away, where Frank's company was stationed.

Two years later, shortly before the regiment's campaign against the Sioux in Montana Territory, Frank was offered a promotion and transfer to one of the companies at Fort Lincoln. He welcomed the increased responsibility, but Katie wrote, "A sudden chill swept over my heart like the touch of cold, invisible fingers, and a curious foreboding enveloped me." Frank deferred to his wife's premonition. Jack Sturgis got the promotion instead.

Katie, Mollie, and their husbands all planned to take leave and visit Philadelphia when the regiment returned from the campaign. They would visit the centennial exposition—celebrating the nation's 100th birthday—and Katie would get to meet Frank's parents, who lived there.

A few weeks after the regiment left, the women at Fort Rice were waiting for news of the campaign. Horn Toad brought it first:

"Custer killed. Whole command killed."

The shocked, white-lipped women did not believe him. They talked late into the night, refusing to believe the whole regiment had been killed, and wondering how Horn Toad could have news before the steamer arrived. At daybreak, the steamer's whistle told them they would soon know.

Unwashed, uncombed, bedraggled from the restless night, they ran to the dock. They clutched their letters, afraid at first to open them. Katie was hysterical with joy when she opened a short letter in which Frank told of the battle, and she noticed another letter from him with a later date. She looked around, and she could tell from the faces that the Fort Rice officers had all survived.

Katie read the second letter. She knew then that all the Fort Lincoln officers, including her sister's husband and Jack Sturgis, who took the transfer Frank had turned down, had been killed. Frank's letter said that he had buried his brother-in-law. It ended, "Poor Mollie, her heart will be completely broken."

While Katie shared her sister's sorrow, she was grateful that Frank had listened to her curious foreboding.

Suggested reading: Katherine Gibson Fougera, *With Custer's Cavalry*, (Caldwell, Idaho: Caxton Printers, 1940).

# WHERE HE WAS, WAS HOME TO ME

When Martha Dunham left her Nantucket Island home for two years of study abroad in German Literature and Music, she fell in love with the splendor of military uniforms. She lived with the family of a former general, a stadt commander in the Franco-Prussian War. His wife warned Martha, "Life in the Army is not always so brilliant. Often it is but 'glittering misery.'" Nevertheless, upon returning in March, 1874, the 28-year-old descendant of Puritans and Quakers married John Summerhayes, her "old friend Jack," eleven years older.

Jack Summerhayes, a short man—five feet, five inches—with ice-blue eyes, had been a whaler and a trapper before service with the Massachusetts Infantry in the Civil War. A captain and a brevet major, Jack Summerhayes was commissioned in the regular army shortly after the war. When he married he had been a second lieutenant for seven years and was stationed at Fort D. A. Russell in Cheyenne with the 8th Infantry.

Martha had never been west of New York, but she liked Fort Russell and Cheyenne. She loved guard mount and cavalry drill—Fort Russell had both cavalry and infantry—as well as orchestra concerts and drives to town. Within three months, the regiment was transferred to Arizona Territory.

After a railroad trip to San Francisco and a steamer trip down the Pacific and up the Gulf of California, they reached the mouth of the Colorado River, where three soldiers died from the heat. They went up the river on barges towed by a stern-wheeler. After leaving two companies at Fort Yuma, they continued upriver, reaching Camp Mojave on September 8, after enduring temperatures ranging from 107 to 122.

Most of the men marched from Camp Mojave, but Martha rode in a Dougherty wagon, commonly called an ambulance. Her first night out was her first under canvas. Just before sunset, some soldiers killed a rattlesnake. Some of the officers and most of the women slept on camp cots, but Martha found the ground more comfortable. Her mattress was laid on a buffalo robe, encircled with a hair rope to keep the snakes away. More troops left at Fort Whipple, near the territorial capital. This would be the headquarters of the regiment. Company K would be posted at Camp Apache in the far eastern part of the territory.

Another company was left at Camp Verde. As the two remaining companies marched on into the Mogollon Mountains, the air cooled and Martha found the stove in their tent handy for dressing in the morning. The only women left in the detachment were another officer's wife plus two or three laundresses.

As they climbed, Martha marveled at the spectacular scenery but wondered if anyone in their right mind would endure the journey just to see it. She was shocked at the dreadful curses of the teamsters. Each mule had a feminine name which "brought the swearing down to a sort of personal basis." Martha's blood curdled and shivers ran up her back as she "half expected to see those teamsters struck down by the hand of the almighty."

As they entered Apache country, Martha was more frightened than she had ever been before. One night five or six officers plus Martha and the other wife sat around their campfire until very late, talking about the danger of Apache attack and the fact that their silhouettes against the fire would make them excellent targets. After Martha and Jack were in their tent, he said she should not worry as Apaches never attack at night.

After their candle was out she asked, "When do they attack?"

"Just before daylight, usually, but don't worry. There aren't any around here."

Martha slept little that night; none at all as dawn approached.

They reached Camp Apache, a post shared with troops of the 5th Cavalry, on October 7, after two months of continuous travel.

Martha and Jack had one room in a log cabin, with a tiny hall to serve as a dining room and a kitchen out back. Their striker—a soldier named Bowen, assigned to do their cooking—brought a stove and cots from the quartermaster, built shelves, and stole a table from somewhere. Martha made curtains for the two small windows in their room.

Jack's Company K had long been a bachelor company. Now that a young woman had joined, the officers and men enjoyed pampering her. At the first party in their tiny quarters, Martha talked to Bowen about the food to cook and serve, and she decided to try making oyster patties herself from a can of Baltimore oysters.

When an officer tasted a patty, he said "Bless my stars! Oyster patties at Camp Apache."

A cavalry captain replied, "They are good." Turning to Bowen, he asked, "Bowen, did you make these?"

The striker drew himself up to his six feet, two inches, snapped his heels, and said, "Yes, sir."

Martha could hear the captain's undertone: "Like hell, he did."

While Martha admired the officers and men of the army, she had nothing but contempt for the Indian Agent. She said, "Of all unkempt, unshorn, disagreeable-looking personages who had ever stepped foot into our quarters, this was the worst."

In January, 1875, Martha gave birth to a baby boy, Harry, the first child born into an officer's family at Camp Apache. A laundress helped for a few days but then had to leave. The soldiers found a Mexican woman in a wood-choppers camp, but neither woman could speak the other's language. On the seventh day a delegation of Indian women came with a beautiful

MARTHA SUMMERHAYES

Arizona Historical Society

cradle. They laced the baby into it as he cooed and chuckled, and the Indian women soothed him to sleep.

When Harry was nine weeks old, Jack was promoted to first lieutenant and transferred to Company C with detached duty at Ehrenberg on the Colorado River. One day there, as she watched a funeral procession where the deceased was wrapped in a white cloth, Martha learned that they had no coffins in the small village. Later she asked Jack to show her the burying ground. He finally took her to a bare, sandy place sprinkled with graves. Some were marked with stones; others with rude wooden crosses. Martha saw deep holes and bones whitening in the sun. Without thinking, she asked Jack what the holes were.

"It's where the coyotes and wolves come in the night."

Martha was horrified.

Martha returned to Nantucket for several months in 1876. She found very little interest in the army back in Massachusetts. A uniform was never seen, and there was no discussion about the Far West. Only her old uncle—a retired whaling captain—showed interest. He had her show him on a map where she had been. Exactly fifty years before, he had sailed into San Francisco Bay on his way to the Arctic Ocean.

In returning to Jack, now at Camp MacDowell, Martha and Harry rode the train to San Francisco (9 days) and on to Los Angeles, a steamer to San Diego, and a stage to Yuma where Jack met her with an army escort. Martha, glad to be back, wrote that she had cast her lot with a soldier and "Where he was, was home to me."

One day Martha was surprised to see her old cook, Bowen, show up. Completing his enlistment, he had gone to San Francisco and lost all his money. He re-enlisted, got assigned to Company C, and again became their cook.

After four years in Arizona, the regiment was transferred to the Department of California. Martha felt like "jumping up onto the table, climbing onto the roof, dancing and singing, and shouting for joy." She spent the summer enjoying the cool breezes of San Francisco while Jack's company campaigned against Bannock Indians in Oregon.

In Fall, 1878, the company was sent to remote Camp MacDermit in northwestern Nevada. It was a colorless, forbidding place, ninety miles north of Winnemucca. It was a one-company post, and the captain's wife was in poor health and confined to her home. Jack was in the field most of the time, and the extreme cold and joyless loneliness depressed Martha.

Paiute chief Winnemucca lived nearby with his family, and he visited Martha from time to time. Gentle and dignified, the old chief enjoyed Martha's sugar cakes. She looked forward to his visits. Four-year-old Harry was her only constant companion during that long, cold, and anxious winter.

She went back to Nantucket in May to stay a year. Her daughter Katherine was born in June, and Jack took a year's leave of absence to join her.

Then Jack's company was transferred to Angel Island in San Francisco Bay. Now Martha and Jack began to truly live. "The flowers ran riot in our garden; fresh fruit and vegetables, fresh fish, and all the luxuries of that marvelous climate were brought to our door." When the fog rolled in and covered the city of St. Francis in its cold vapors, the Island of the Angels lay warm and bright in the sunshine. It seemed a paradise to Martha.

During its second winter on Angel Island, the regiment was ordered back to Arizona to fight Geronimo. The officers packed their evening clothes in camphor and aired out their campaign clothing. But this was a campaign, and the wives were left behind to weep in the "season of gloom. The skies were dull and murky and the rain poured down."

In Fall, 1882, the regiment was back, and Jack's company was transferred to Fort Halleck in northeastern Nevada. Much different from Fort MacDermit, it was just thirteen miles from the overland railroad and backed by magnificent mountains. A combined cavalry-infantry post, it allowed Martha to ride to her heart's content.

Martha spent another two years on Angel Island while the regiment campaigned in Arizona, followed by a hot summer at Fort Lowell, near Tucson. As they looked forward to a pleasant winter, they were transferred to Fort Niobrara in northern Nebraska. There, Martha took her daily promenade only when the temperature rose to eighteen degrees below zero.

Martha met President Cleveland when Jack was the senior lieutenant in the 8th Infantry, having served twenty-two years as a second and first lieutenant. She told the president what she thought of the army's promotion system. In short order Jack, first, and then another 8th Infantry lieutenant were promoted to captains and transferred to the Quartermaster Department.

Jack and Martha were transferred to Santa Fe, from there to Fort Sam Houston in San Antonio, then David's Island in New York Harbor, followed by Jefferson Barracks in St. Louis, and Fort Myer in Virginia. In the Spanish-American War Jack was promoted to major and sent to New York to take charge of the Army Transport Service. He retired as a lieutenant colonel in 1900, and he and Martha moved back to Nantucket.

Jack died there in 1911, and Martha followed two months later. Jack's home had been her home for many years and in many places.

Suggested reading: Martha Summerhayes, *Vanished Arizona* (Lincoln: University of Nebraska, 1979.)

52

# SHE DROVE BEST UNDER A STORMY WIND

Richard Henry Dana met Jessie Benton Frémont in 1859, and he described her in *Two Years Before the Mast* as "a heroine equal to either fortune—the salons of Paris and the drawing rooms of New York and Washington—or the roughest life of the remote and wild." "She was true blue," he said, "full of courage and talent." The *New York Tribune* on October 11, 1861, said she was "not only a historic woman, but the greatest woman in America."

In 1841, when Jessie Benton was seventeen, she told her parents she wanted to marry John C. Frémont, an army officer whom she had known about two years. But Frémont was what the public called a bastard. His mother was married to a man old enough to be her grandfather when her baby was born. The baby's father was Charles Frémon, a Frenchman who taught his native language at William and Mary and other schools in Virginia.

Jessie's father, Thomas Hart Benton, had represented Missouri in the United States Senate since it had become a state. Then serving in his fourth term, he was one of America's most powerful men. When her parents said "no" to the marriage, Jessie eloped to marry the man she loved. He was twenty-eight, although Jessie never learned his age until six years later.

By the next year Jessie was back in the good graces of her parents, and her husband was making the first of his five exploratory journeys west. Jessie helped him write the reports of those journeys, which made him famous as an explorer and map maker of the early West. He surveyed and mapped more of the Old West than did Lewis and Clark.

Frémont had ability and imagination and was, at times, very popular. But he was impulsive and often made poor judgments. He needed a wife like Jessie. Clever, bold, ambitious, and controversial, she was always his greatest fan.

On Frémont's third expedition, he got caught in the middle of a powerplay resulting from the conquest of California in the War against Mexico. Naval Commodore Robert Stockton appointed Lieutenant Colonel Frémont military governor of California. But Brigadier General Stephen Kearny also had orders from Washington and he thought he should be the governor. Accepting the appointment from the man he thought had the power to grant it necessarily made Frémont disobey the order of a superior in his own branch of the service. Frémont was allowed to march his men back to the United States, but when they reached Fort Leavenworth in August, 1847, Kearny put him under arrest and directed him to continue on to Washington for a court martial on charges of mutiny.

Jessie met her husband in Westport for a warm reunion after the

JESSIE BENTON FRÉMONT

Arizona Historical Society

absence of over two years. They continued on to Washington together. Jessie immediately wrote to President Polk, complaining that she feared important witnesses would be transferred and not available for cross examination. The witnesses were present, although Frémont had to cross examine them himself. His civilian attorneys, Jessie's father and his own brother-in-law, were only allowed to serve as advisors.

Jessie was present every day of the trial, which started November 2. However, by December she had a bad cold which almost became pneumonia. She was expecting her second child, and her doctor ordered her to stay home. She listened carefully as her father and her husband related each day's events.

On January 31 the court found Frémont guilty and sentenced him to dismissal from the army. But six of the court's twelve members recommended clemency. President Polk approved the sentence but remitted the penalty, and he ordered Frémont to duty in Mexico. Both Jessie and her husband thought that his remaining in the army would admit the justice of the court's finding, so he resigned his commission.

Frémont bought a forty thousand acre land grant from a former governor of Mexican California. Much gold was discovered, but his title did not include minerals; nor did it describe specific boundaries that could be located on the ground. As a result, although Frémont was at one time very rich, in the long run the *Las Mariposas* became a constant headache, drawing away his funds.

Frémont became one of California's first senators, just as his father-in-law had in Missouri.

Frémont's popularity and his interest in politics brought him a bid from the Democratic party to be their candidate for president in 1856. He turned them down. Then the newly-created Republican party asked. This time he accepted and became the party's first presidential candidate. His running mate, Senator William L. Dayton of New Jersey, beat out Abraham Lincoln for the vice presidential nomination.

As expected, Jessie took an active part in what some called the Frémont and Jessie Campaign. She was the first wife of a presidential candidate to appear in public with him as part of his campaign. At a rally in New Hampshire, Frémont's name was left off a banner which read, "Jessie for the White House." She supervised all the campaign correspondence. Many baby girls, born during the campaign, were named Jessie Ann.

When Frémont's illegitimacy became an ugly issue, Jessie researched his family history. His mother descended from an aristocratic Virginia family, related to George Washington. Her father, a wealthy landowner, was a prominent member of the Virginia House of Burgesses. Jessie claimed that Frémont's mother and her husband were granted a divorce by the state legislature, following which she married his father, and the ex-husband, seventy-six, married his housekeeper. But she could find no public record of a divorce, a later marriage, or even her husband's birth.

The governor of Virginia, in a campaign speech for Buchanan, said, "The hoisting of the black Republican flag by a Frenchman's bastard was an overt act, amounting to a declaration of civil war."

Frèmont's religion even became a campaign issue. He had been raised an Episcopalian, confirmed at fourteen. But when he married the daughter of the prominent senator, they could not find a Protestant pastor to perform the ceremony, so they were married by a Catholic priest. Henry Ward Beecher, America's most prominent Protestant clergyman, said during the campaign that if he had been in Frémont's place, "We would have been married if it had required us to walk through a row of priests and bishops as long as from Washington to Rome, winding up with the Pope himself."

The campaign exhausted Jessie, but she still took time away to have her portrait painted. After five pregnancies, her face and figure had thickened, but the painter made her girlishly slender. "It resembles me," Jessie said of the portrait with a sigh, "as the dew resembles rain."

Senator Benton was too fervent a Democrat to vote for a Republican, even for his son-in-law, whom he admired greatly. Jessie deplored the painful rift between the two most important men in her life, but she desperately wanted her husband to win.

He almost did. He carried eleven of the sixteen free states, but Buchanan carried Illinois, Pennsylvania, and Indiana, and, with the exception of Maryland, which voted for Fillmore, he carried the entire South. In a split among three candidates, Frémont was a close second to Buchanan. The Know-Nothing candidate, Millard Fillmore, ran a distant third.

The antagonism between North and South was heated, and many predicted that the Republican party would win in 1860, with secession following even if it meant civil war. That, of course, is what happened.

When the Civil War broke out, Frémont—by then a millionaire—was appointed one of the Union's first four major generals. He was made commander of the Department of the West—Illinois and all the states and territories between the Mississippi and the Rockies—with headquarters in St. Louis. But the town, once so hospitable to the Frémonts and the Bentons, was now sullen and hostile. Confederate flags flew everywhere and recruiting for the Confederate Army was the main business. It was the metropolis of a state about evenly divided on the issues of slavery and secession.

As Frémont struggled to secure equipment, arms, and supplies, and fight off Confederate troops, he decided that a bold, decisive stroke was necessary to save Missouri for the Union. So on August 30, 1861, he signed an Emancipation Order liberating the slaves of all the rebels in the

56

state. One might accept the distinction between slaves of rebels and other slaves, who were not liberated, because the order was part of a decision to confiscate the property of rebels who were fighting the established government. Yet the idea that a military officer could determine the political rights of others seems as strange as an army officer obeying a naval officer which put him in direct disobedience of his own superior. Jessie, however, was enthusiastic about the proclamation. She was often called General Jessie for her role as her husband's chief aide and confidant.

President Lincoln was not so enthusiastic. Up until then the war was about preserving the union. Sixteen months would pass before Lincoln freed the slaves. In the meantime he knew that something had to be done about one of his four top generals, a loose cannon in the west.

Before Lincoln could act, Jessie was in the White House with a letter explaining the situation in the west. When Lincoln met her at nine p. m. in the red parlor, she was exhausted. She had ridden the railroad common cars for two days and nights, and had not taken time to change her clothing upon arrival. Without asking her to sit down, Lincoln read the letter she handed him. Then he said, "It was a war for a great national idea, the Union. Your husband should not have dragged the Negro into it."

The president said he would send Jessie her answer the next day, but nothing came. She sent another letter asking if she could have the first letter back along with copies of the charges against her husband. She never got them. Lincoln called her, "That political female."

In October, Lincoln removed Frémont from command. Both Jessie and her husband were devastated. Some of his staff officers were also relieved, without pay. But Jessie kept her spirits up. "I am a deeply built ship," she often said. "I drive best under a stormy wind."

The Frémonts went to *Las Mariposas* in April, 1858. Jessie learned that two days before they reached San Francisco, her father had died of prostate cancer.

In 1855 the state supreme court had confirmed Frémont's title, but the description merely referred to a large area between three rivers and the Sierra Nevada. Frémont drew the boundaries to his sixty square miles so that they included rich mines claimed and worked by others. In the 1856 election he only got six percent of the vote in Mariposa County, none at all in some mining precincts.

The bitterness came to a head in July, when angry miners took possession of one mine and put Frémont's miners under siege in another. During the standoff, Jesse rode a wagon to the village saloon serving as the enemy's headquarters, and defied them to shoot her in the back as she rode away.

The crisis ended with an agreement that State Governor John B.

Weller could decide the issue of possession. He was the widower of a Benton cousin, so the enemy miners gave up.

John Charles Frémont, beloved by many and hated by a few, had one more moment in the nation's spotlight. In 1878, President Rutherford B. Hayes appointed him governor of Arizona Territory. By this time the family fortune was gone, and Jessie helped pay the bills by writing children's stories and magazine articles.

Frémont's yearly salary was only $2600, and he made it clear when he accepted the position that it would give him the time and opportunity to find investments that would restore his fortune. Now he could dream big again!

He recommended building a railroad from Tucson through Mexico to a port on the Gulf of California. He tried to buy a large ranch in Mexico. His grandest proposal was to harness the Colorado River and irrigate a large basin, now the rich Imperial Valley of Southern California. His activities kept him in the saddle some days for twelve hours without a let up. Many times he was away from Arizona for extended trips to seek Eastern investment money.

Three of the Frémonts' five children survived infancy. Both boys became military officers, and one of them, with tuberculosis, went west with his parents. The son's lungs cleared up, but the climate in Prescott, the capital, did not agree with Jessie. She took a house in New York to continue her literary career.

Realizing how much he missed his wife, Frémont moved his office to Tucson so that she might come back. Plans for that were underway when citizens began complaining about Frémont's absences from the Territory. With a new president in office in 1881, Frémont resigned.

Now sixty-eight, his hair turned white, the old explorer, map maker, and dreamer of big dreams returned east to join his beloved Jessie. They had nine more years together. By then four counties and seven towns in eight states had been named Fremont.

Jessie survived her husband by twelve years. Congress voted her a widow's pension, and the women of Los Angeles bought her a small cottage there. She saw to it that her husband's story was told over and over. Anyone foolish enough to criticize him got a well-deserved public scolding from the woman who thrived in stormy weather.

Suggested reading: Pamela Herr, *Jessie Benton Frémont* (New York: Franklin Watts, 1987).

# HERO'S WIFE

**W**hen Alice (Allie) Blackwood was nine, her father moved the family from Michigan to California, hoping his wife's health would improve. But the mother died in two years, and Allie and her sister were sent back to live with an uncle and aunt.

Uncle Robert and Aunt Becky sent Allie to a Young Ladies Seminary where she learned to be a proper wife and mother. But the high adventure already packed into her life, coupled with her independent mind and many talents, made it difficult to fit the Victorian mold.

In 1863, when Allie was eighteen, she met Frank Baldwin, a lieutenant in the Michigan Volunteers who had just been paroled in a Civil War exchange of prisoners. Allie remembered the soldiers who had escorted her wagon train to California and was impressed by the gallant warrior in his glittering braid.

Both Allie and Frank were told that a wife should give background support for her husband. This would produce internal conflict in any marriage between an independent, talented woman and a traditional, Victorian-type man. What complicated the issue for the Baldwins was that for most of his army career, Frank was the army's greatest hero.

Only two regular army soldiers have each received two Medals of Honor. The first—Tom Custer—was killed in 1876, just two years after Frank got his second medal. So from 1876 until he died forty-seven years later at age eighty-one, Frank Baldwin was clearly the army's greatest living hero. This produced conflict between the intense, loving relationship of Allie and Frank and the public face each put on their marriage.

After the Civil War—where he won the first Medal of Honor at Peach Tree Creek, Georgia—Frank failed at farming, and he did not like college. In February, 1866, he got a second lieutenancy in the regular army. An incident on Christmas night of that year shows Frank's courage and determination. He was riding alone at night toward his post at Fort Ellsworth, Kansas, when a pack of wolves attacked. Armed only with a pistol and about fifty cartridges, he forced his horse through heavy snow while shooting back at the wolves. Whenever he dropped one, the others would tear at its body, giving Frank and his horse more breathing room. When he crossed the last creek and saw the fort's lights, his horse fell dead. Frank had less than ten cartridges when he staggered into the fort.

On January 10, 1867, Frank and Allie were married. Although average in height at five feet, eight inches, Frank was trim and muscular. With his handsome features and self confident attitude, Allie thought him a dashing officer. Allie, too, was average in height, slim and well proportioned. She had dark hair and pretty features. Her only blemish was decayed teeth, but she kept her mouth closed as much as she could.

Frank wrote in his diary a few days before the wedding: "The more I see her the more I love her. She seems perfectly contented to go away with me. How much ought I try to make such a worthy lady happy. Nothing shall be left undone that will add to her happiness."

Aunt Becky's advice to her niece was pure Victorian: "Bear and forebear! A coachman who had known Allie for years said most of the wedding guests were thinking: "Allie sure needs halterbreaking!"

Frank's quarters at Fort Ellsworth were a two room dugout in a creek bank. A blanket partitioned the "drawing room" with its rough plank floor into a living room and a bedroom. The kitchen had a dirt floor. They ate their first evening at the officers mess. The commissary sergeant's wife tried to console Allie, but she broke down and cried. A month passed before Frank could write, "Allie is very cheerful and very happy today."

The soldiers were building the permanent fort a short distance away, and the officers moved into semi-private quarters in the spring. The Baldwins had one large room across the hall from a major and his wife and baby. Neither unit had a kitchen, so the major's family and the Baldwins shared a kitchen tent in the rear.

Daughter Juanita was born in Trinidad, Colorado, in October, 1867, while Frank was being transferred to Fort Wingate in New Mexico Territory. The labor was difficult, and Allie had to rest nine days before they could move on. After that she dreaded the thought of having another child. She was sure it would kill her.

Fort Wingate was a post of hardship. The soldiers drank heavily and desertion rates were high. The women were quarrelsome and barely spoke to each other. Allie missed the companionship of Fort Ellsworth.

In February, 1869, Frank decided that Allie and the baby should go to Michigan until he was reassigned. When she reached Hays City, Kansas, she took a room in a hotel where the partitions only reached halfway to the ceiling and one of them had a large hole through which men peered at the new tenants. A black soldier from the 10th Cavalry had carried her bags, and he promised to stand watch by her door that night.

A scuffle outside woke Allie. She heard shots, the door flew open, and the black man fell dead at her feet. She sat up the rest of the night.

Six months later Allie rejoined Frank at Fort Hays, but court martial duty in Santa Fe and other assignments brought frequent separations, producing discord. Allie was an excellent singer, and she had dreamed about a professional career. She complained to Frank about never having a higher career than "singing always at home." At this time she had all her teeth pulled and dentures fitted.

The Baldwins began having violent arguments. Each time he came home from a separation he tried to re-establish a dominant relationship, only to be rebuffed by an assertive wife. Once she locked herself in the bedroom and Frank kicked the door down. Another time she swung at him. He packed her bags for Michigan, but tempers cooled.

While Frank struggled with his professional goals—he wanted the cavalry where advancement opportunities were greater—and he and Allie struggled with their personal problems, the Cheyennes, Comanches, and Kiowas began raiding the Southern Plains, particularly in western Indian Territory and the Texas Panhandle. Nelson Miles, commander of the 5th Infantry, was put in charge of a five-column thrust to restore order. In July, 1874, he made Frank his chief of scouts.

Frank killed the first Indian in the Red River War of 1874, and his daring conduct brought him front page newspaper coverage throughout the country and his second Medal of Honor.

Back in Michigan, even before she knew what Frank had done, Allie's letter to him revealed her love, fear, pride, and, perhaps, envy:

"I have always known you were brave. You are living a life fraught with peril and excitement. Your mental and physical powers are kept in constant service. And you are living the life you love. Now look at me! I an a woman with all the love and anxiety of a wife for the man she loves. I have no stirring scenes to pass through. There are no eventful episodes in my existence. I am not living the life I love. I have nothing to do but watch and wait."

A week later, after she had learned what Frank had done, she wrote: "I felt as if it must be some fiction. Frank, you are a big lion among your friends here and your name is prominently mentioned among the papers. Don't for mercy's sake, ever run such a risk again as you did when you undertook that journey with only three scouts. I don't care for all the orders or generals in creation. I am the one to suffer and mourn and not they."

One of Frank's letters to Allie suggests some of his motivation: "This morning I discovered a band of 200 warriors whom I have attacked and, after a hard fight of 4 ½ hours, completely routed. Gen. Miles came up tonight and is well pleased with my victory. Says it is the most complete yet won during the war. Are you proud of me now?"

Allie did not go with Frank in 1876 when the 5th Infantry was sent to Montana Territory for action against the Indians who had defeated Custer. When they were reunited at Fort Leavenworth, Allie said she had been requested to sing at a benefit for the German girls. These were two frontier girls, captured by Indians, whose rescue was largely the result of Frank's heroism in the Red River War.

Frank hated the public display of his wife's talents. He even lectured her about the proper role of a wife: "Feel, my darling that you can by your interests in me and my welfare do a great deal to aid me."

Allie responded: "My miserable ambitions, proud nature and disposition is the cause of my unhappiness. I would be someone if I had a chance, but with neither money, influence, or beauty, which is everything in a woman, what hope have I but of dragging along in the rut as long as I live?  Everyone names 'Baldwin' as the best one in the regiment.  Who ever hears of me?  No one.  And when something offers a small chance to appear in a good light, you object."

In November, 1876, a depressed Allie wrote: I feel very despondent and melancholy most of the time as if there was not much to enjoy in life and less in the future.  I have had enough, God knows, of living on the frontier, and you know I did not have much happiness in those days.  I wish you were out of the regiment.  Aside from you and Nita, I have not a single thing to live for."

Allie recovered from her depression and lived with Frank in Montana.  Once, during one of Frank's frequent absences, she was out riding with another captain when horse thieves attacked.  Allie was bent low over her sidesaddle, ducking bullets flying over her head, when her saddle girth broke.

"What shall I do now?" she shouted to the captain.

"Let it drop and ride a-straddle."

In her frantic efforts to keep her skirt down, Allie was making a public display of what she called her "nether extremities."

"Don't look at me," she shouted.

"Never mind your legs, I've got to get you home."

The captain deposited her at her door, bedraggled, skinned, covered with blisters, disheveled, and ragged.

The army gave Frank a year's tour of Europe, which Allie enjoyed. After more service in Oregon, Montana (again), North Dakota, Texas, Chicago, Washington, and the Phillippines, Frank retired to Colorado in 1906.

Frank decided to establish a small farm near Denver.

"General," his hired man once said, tired of his many orders.  "You may know a lot about war but you don't know about farming."

Refusing to tolerate insubordination, Frank fired the man and his second attempt at farming also failed.

In 1921, when he was seventy-nine, Frank attended the burial of the unknown soldier at Arlington Cemetery.  Two years later, he was buried there, himself.

In 1930, eighty-five-year-old Allie was buried at his side.  She closed her memoirs saying they had had a long march together.

Suggested reading: Robert H. Steinbach, *A Long March* (Austin: University of Texas, 1989).

## ORDERING INFORMATION

True Tales of the Old West
is projected for 38 volumes.

For Titles in Print,
Ask at your bookstore
or write:

PIONEER PRESS
P. O. Box 216
Carson City, NV 89702-0216
Voice Phone (775) 888-9867
FAX (775) 888-0908

Other titles in progress include:

Frontier Artists
Californios
Western Duelists
Early Lumbermen
Frontier Militiamen
Frontier Teachers

Ghosts & Mysteries

Doctors & Healers
Old West Merchants
Scientists & Engineers
Visitors to the Frontier